3

BALLROOM DANCING

STEP-BY-STEP

BALLROOM DANCING

STEP-BY-STEP

learn to waltz, quickstep, foxtrot, tango and jive in over 400 easy-to-follow colour photographs and diagrams

Paul Bottomer

southwater

This edition is published by Southwater
an imprint of Anness Publishing Ltd
Hermes House, 88–89 Blackfriars Road, London SE1 8HA
tel. 020 7401 2077; fax 020 7633 9499
www.southwaterbooks.com; www.annesspublishing.com

If you like the images in this book and would like to investigate using
them for publishing, promotions or advertising, please visit our website
www.practicalpictures.com for more information.

© Anness Publishing Ltd 2006, 2008

UK agent: The Manning Partnership Ltd; tel. 01225 478444;
fax 01225 478440; sales@manning-partnership.co.uk
UK distributor: Grantham Book Services Ltd; tel. 01476 541080;
fax 01476 541061; orders@gbs.tbs-ltd.co.uk
North American agent/distributor: National Book Network;
tel. 301 459 3366; fax 301 429 5746; www.nbnbooks.com
Australian agent/distributor: Pan Macmillan Australia; tel. 1300 135 113;
fax 1300 135 103; customer.service@macmillan.com.au
New Zealand agent/distributor: David Bateman Ltd;
tel. (09) 415 7664; fax (09) 415 8892

A CIP catalogue record for this book is available from the British Library.
Publisher: Joanna Lorenz
Editorial Director: Helen Sudell
Editors: Lindsay Porter and Elizabeth Woodland
Photographer: John Freeman
Clothes Stylist: Leeann Mackenie
Hair and Make-up: Karen Kennedy
Designers: Clare Baggaley and Mark Stevens
Cover Designer: Balley Design Associates
Production Controller: Lee Sargent

Previously published as part of a larger volume, *Dance Class*

ETHICAL TRADING POLICY
Because of our ongoing ecological investment programme, you, as our
customer, can have the pleasure and reassurance of knowing that a tree
is being cultivated on your behalf to naturally replace the materials used
to make the book you are holding. For further information about this
scheme, go to www.annesspublishing.com/trees

Acknowledgements
The author and publisher would like to thank the following for their
contribution to this book:

Simon Selmon and Derek Young, F&Exam. UKA for their expert advice
on Lindy Hop and Rock 'n' Roll respectively.

Many thanks to the following dancers for their participation in the
photographic sequences. Their expertise and enthusiasm were
invaluable.
Elaine Bottomer (four times undefeated World & European Tango
Argentino Supreme Champion and All-England Professional Ballroom
Championship Grand Finalist), Goran and Nicola Nordin (UK Professional
Latin-American Champions), Harm-Jan Schadenberg and Wendy Kroeze
(three times undefeated Dutch Professional Latin-American Champions),
John Byrnes and Jane Lyttleton (UK Professional Rising Star Latin-
American Champions), Mark and Jane Shutlar, Steve and Deborah
McCormick, Jeff and Teresa Lindley, Michael Burton, Camilla Laitalia,
Trevor and Naomi Ironmonger, Karina Rebello, Berg Dias, Andrew Barrett,
Luis Bittencourt, Tanya Janes, Mina di Placido, Phillippe Laue, Julie
Glover, Mark Field, Natascha Hall, Katherine Porter, Anny Ho, Ben Ryley,
Shahriar Shariat, Debbie Smith, Debbie Watson, Simon Selmon, Helia
Lloyd and Dr Eric Sille.

Many thanks to Supadance International for supplying dance shoes
for photography.

Dresses were very kindly lent by After 6, Consortium, Pineapple,
Tadashi and Vera Mont.

Contents

Introduction

Dancing is both the most artistic of social pastimes and the most social of artistic pastimes. In all societies, dancing forms an integral part of the lifestyle. Dancing is not only a reflection of life but is a basic human expression of life itself. While the initial motivation to dance is often a social one, once past the hurdle of actually learning to dance, many find in the music, the atmosphere and the dance, the opportunity to take on a new persona. In an instant, the dancer can be mentally and emotionally transported to almost any scenario of their choosing – an elegant Gala Ball in Vienna, a smart dinner dance in London's West End, a New York night spot or a Parisian café. The music and venue create the atmosphere but it is the dancer who expresses their own individuality through the language of the dance.

In this unique volume, the most internationally popular ballroom dances are explained in a practical and easily understandable way. The descriptions used in this book represent a simplified version of the internationally standardized style and technique used throughout the world. These dances include the Social Foxtrot, Waltz, Quickstep, Slow Foxtrot, Modern Tango and Jive. There is no uniformly standardized technique for Viennese Waltz, so in this book it is presented as an easy style enjoyed by ordinary social dancers rather than the more demanding style danced in championships.

Whatever your musical taste or individual preferences, the huge variety of dances ensures that there is something to suit you. You do not need to be a good dancer to enjoy the dancing, the music, the mood, the atmosphere and, of course, the social life. Dancing is accessible to everyone irrespective of age or ability.

Dancing is a fabulous way of keeping fit both physically and mentally and is recommended by the medical profession. Most people with disabilities are able to enjoy and benefit from it, but if you have a condition which would prevent you from taking a brisk walk, you should consult your medical practitioner before embarking on your dance programme.

As you work through the book, relax and learn steadily at your own pace. If necessary, read through the relevant section several times until you become totally familiar with the move. Remember too that some of the most important information is in the introductory section to each dance. Focus on what you know rather than what you don't and avoid setting your expectations too high in too short a timescale. Everyone needs time. To make progress in any style of dancing, you will need commitment, application and as much practice as possible but the rewards for these can deeply enrich the quality of life in so many varied and worthwhile ways. And the great thing is that it's so much fun! So, enjoy this introduction to some of the world's most popular dances and remember the sooner you learn to dance, the longer you'll have to enjoy it. It won't be long before you, like so many others, have become completely dance crazy!

On the Floor

The dance floor, whether crowded or not, is a very valuable asset and should be treated, like its users, with the utmost respect.

Always walk around the edge of the floor and never across it, especially while people are dancing. The sudden emergence of a bystander trying to dodge dancers can cause chaos on the floor and is an unnecessary and discourteous hazard to the dancers.

When taking to the floor, it is important to avoid causing problems to the dancers who are already there. Since men normally start a dance facing the outside of the room, it may seem quite natural for them to walk onto the floor backwards while their attention is focused on their

Take up the starting position only when you have assessed the situation on the dance floor. Do not dance onto the floor as this may hinder other dancers.

Waltz Music

Waltz music is organized with three beats to each bar of music. The Basic Waltz is also organized into sections of three steps. Each step therefore corresponds to a single beat of music. Musically, the first beat in each bar is accentuated or emphasized and it is on this beat that you should start to dance. While the beat is giving a count of 1-2-3, you should be dancing the walk-side-close movements of the Basic Waltz.

The time signature of a waltz is 3/4 with a tempo currently recommended internationally as 30 bars per minute. This means that it takes only two seconds to dance each section of the Waltz. This is in fact a relatively easy pace which you can really enjoy.

partner. As this will cause a hindrance to the dancers, it is far better to approach the floor and assess the flow of floor traffic before taking up your starting position with due consideration to the other dancers.

When leaving the floor, especially during the course of a dance, the same consideration should be shown. If you are finishing during the dance, you should dance to the edge of the floor, leave the floor at that point and walk back around the perimeter to return to your seat.

The Dance Floor

Before you begin the steps, here are some basic ways of orientating yourself in the room.

• The flow of the floor traffic (the dancers) will be in an anticlockwise (counterclockwise) direction around the room.
• The orientation of the dancers will be described in relation to the nearest wall, the centre line of the floor and in terms of zigs and zags.

Going with the flow

Assuming that the room is rectangular, stand adjacent to any wall, making sure the wall is on the man's right and the woman's left. The man will now be in a position to move forward with the flow of floor traffic and the woman to move backwards. In some steps, the man will face against the flow of traffic with the wall on his left-hand side. The overall movement of the figure being danced will, however, continue to go with the flow.

The centre line

Still in the same position, the centre line of the room will be on the man's left and the woman's right.

Zigs and zags

A diagonal line, which we will call a "zig", extends from the centre line to the wall parallel to it at an angle of approximately 45°. Another diagonal line, a "zag", extends from the wall to the centre line at an angle of approximately 45°. In the Basic Waltz and Quickstep, the man moves forward along the zigs and backwards along the zags in order to "tack" along the room. Conversely, the woman moves backwards along the zigs and forward along the zags, opposite her partner, as they both travel with the flow. All the Standard Partner dances are described using the

same method. Remember that, as you dance around the room, you will encounter corners and will need to accommodate them.

Cornering

When you turn a corner, you will orientate yourself using the new wall and the centre line, which is always parallel to the wall you are using. The zigs and zags run along the diagonals between the new centre line and the new wall as before. The flow will, of course, flow around the corner.

The diagram illustrates the main ways in which the dancers orientate themselves in the room. You can start to get used to this by practising at home.

The Hold

When taking up a hold for the Waltz, Quickstep and Slow Foxtrot, the man takes the woman's right hand in his left hand and draws her to him. This enables him to place her slightly to his right. When in the correct position, the buttons on the man's shirt should be opposite the woman's right shoulder.

To take up the hold, the man presents his left hand as if he is a policeman stopping traffic. The woman then places the hooked middle finger of her right hand between the thumb and forefinger of the man's left hand, palm to palm. Next, the woman places her forefinger and third finger on top of her middle finger and finally rests her little finger on top of the others, curling her thumb around the man's thumb. The joined hands should be held just below eye-level with the hand-hold and arms firm but not rigid. The man now places the fingertips of his left hand along the edge of the woman's right hand with the fingers pointing to the floor. In this way, the underside of both the man's left wrist and the woman's right wrist are facing the floor. When you start to dance, this will considerably enhance stability and make leading much easier.

The hold (front view).

The man cups the woman's left shoulder blade with his right hand, with the fingertips ideally placed against the woman's spine. The woman straightens the fingers of her left hand but allows the thumb to extend out in its normal position. She then places her left hand on the man's upper arm with a straight and flat wrist. It is unnecessary for her third and little fingers to be resting on the man's arm. Both the man and the woman should hold their elbows slightly forward of their backs and a little away from the body. The shoulders should be relaxed, never tensed or hunched.

The man and woman should both stand upright, lifting the diaphragm to produce a good posture. The man and woman

The hold (rear view).

maintain lower diaphragm and upper stomach contact throughout much of the dance. They should hold their heads a little to the left and with the chin up. The weight of the head can have an adverse effect on balance if it is not held in the desired position. Do not look at your feet. The man's back and arms provide a "frame" in which the woman is held. A good frame is essential for good dancing and good leading.

The hold and starting position often feel too rigid to a first-time dancer for fluidity of movement, but with a little practice, a good but relaxed posture and hold can be developed. This is one of the main skills which characterize a partner who is easy to dance with. The frame created by the man's arms and reinforced by his back and diaphragm should be held still and firm, that is to say that the arms should never move independently of the body. Once this is achieved, the woman will be able to feel a clear lead.

Much of the process of leading is not something which the man does actively but is rather the result of clear and positive dancing. The best leading is the sort which leaves the woman no other option but to dance what the man intends without her really having to think about it. Once the woman has to work at following, the enjoyment is largely lost for her. The woman should accept the man's lead and not try to guess what he will do next and commit herself to a course of action which might be the wrong one.

The woman has a responsibility when she is moving forward and the man is moving back. Since she is the one who can see where the couple are moving, she must indicate to the man if they are about to dance into a problem. She can do this by squeezing the thumb and middle finger of her left hand and then allowing the man to lead his evasive manoeuvre.

This position shows the frame created by the man's arms. The arms, back and diaphragm all move with one another – no element moves independently. This provides the frame with which to lead the woman.

The woman indicates tactical problems with a slight pressure of the left hand.

Legs and Feet

It may seem surprising to leave comment on these until last. However, we dance with the whole of our bodies and, once the body is working properly, the feet and legs will often largely take care of themselves. Knees are very important and you will feel more comfortable, relaxed and in control if you can keep your knees flexed at all times. Dancing, in a basic sense, is not so very different from walking and yet it is so often the case that someone who can walk perfectly well feels challenged when taking a normal walk forward, simply because they are "dancing" and not walking down the street.

Try not to get too far away from your partner or worry about stepping on their feet. As the woman is positioned slightly to the man's right, when he walks forward with the right foot his foot will go between the woman's feet. When he walks forward with the left foot he will be walking outside the woman. The same occurs when the woman is moving forward and the man is moving backwards. Using this helpful technique, there is very little chance of treading on a partner's foot unless you create a gap between you.

Taking a step

When taking a step, move your foot into position and then remember to move your body weight onto that foot.

Which foot to start with

Some teachers teach the Waltz or Quickstep starting with the left foot for the man. Logic suggests that when we are moving forward and want to initiate a turn to the right, we do this by curving the right foot forward. This is a good move to start with because the woman can feel the curve and instinctively knows that, because she is moving backwards, it is natural for her to start moving back with her left foot. If the man were to start with his left foot moving forward and dance no turn, the woman would not have a clear lead.

Left: Try not to get too far away from your partner or worry about stepping on his or her feet. As the woman is positioned slightly to the man's right, when he walks forward with the right foot his foot will go between the woman's feet.

Above and right: When taking a step, move your foot into position and then remember to move your body weight directly onto that foot.

Right: When the man walks forward with the left foot he will be walking outside the woman. The same occurs when the woman is moving forward and the man is moving backwards. Using this technique, there is little chance of treading on a partner's foot.

Floorcraft

Your positioning on the floor and how you progress around it may be likened to driving in a flow of traffic. The skill, experience and thinking ahead necessary to negotiate the other dancers are called floorcraft.

As you get used to dancing around the room it will become apparent that there is more to floorcraft than may at first be obvious. The ability to avoid problems and read the situation ahead of you are both attributes of a good dancer. This ability develops with practice but can be acquired more easily by following a few guidelines, the responsibility for which lies mainly with the man.

• It is extremely important to adhere to the given orientation in the room. If you allow yourself to wander from the prescribed path, it will be very difficult to get back to it.

• If you are following a couple around a corner, stay behind and on the wall side of them. By the time you reach their position, they will usually have moved on.

• Avoid dancing across a corner if a couple are already in the corner. You risk them running into you as they exit the corner.

• Women, even though trying to help, should not attempt to lead the man.

All the figures described in this book have been selected not only for their attractiveness as easily enjoyable figures but also for their usefulness as floorcraft figures. As your repertoire grows, so will your ability first to avoid problems and then to escape from any further difficulties.

Floorcraft skills basically entail manoeuvring around obstacles, rather like negotiating through traffic. As you become accustomed to moving around the dance floor, your style will become more relaxed and flowing.

Social Foxtrot

For many, the ability just to get on to the dance floor and move around it comfortably, confidently and inconspicuously is a worthy aim in itself. This version of the Foxtrot provides an easily repeatable basic movement which first-time dancers can quickly enjoy dancing. Despite being designated a Foxtrot, this dance has been designed to be enjoyed to a wide and varied range of music; from Blues to Quickstep, from Tango to Rock 'n' Roll and even some current chart music. In fact, you can dance the Social Foxtrot to almost any tune with a 2/4 or 4/4 time signature, which means virtually any dance music except that in Waltz-time. The tempo, though, will vary according to the particular style of music.

Take up the Standard Ballroom hold but, for this dance, you can afford to make it a little more informal and relaxed. The Social Foxtrot is a compact dance, ideal for crowded floors, so keep all the steps small. Start on a zig. The man is standing on his right foot, feet together, and the woman corresponds, standing on her left foot.

Basic Movement

1

COUNT – SLOW

Man Walk forward with the left foot along the zig.

Woman Walk back with the right foot along the zig.

2

COUNT – SLOW

Man Walk forward with the right foot along the zig starting to turn from the zig to the zag.

Woman Walk back with the left foot along the zig starting to walk from the zig to the zag.

3

COUNT – QUICK

Man Move the left foot to the side, turning from the zig to the zag.

Woman Move the right foot to the side, a small step, turning from the zig to the zag.

4

COUNT – QUICK

Man Close the right foot to the left foot. End standing on the right foot, backing along the zag.

Woman Close the left foot to the right foot. End standing on the left foot, facing along the zag.

5

COUNT – SLOW

Man Walk back with the left foot along the zag.

Woman Walk forward with the right foot along the zag.

Style Tip

Keep your knees and elbows relaxed, take small and comfortable steps throughout, and enjoy feeling and expressing the rhythm.

6

COUNT – SLOW

Man Walk back with the right foot along the zag.

Woman Walk forward with the left foot along the zag.

7

COUNT – QUICK

Man Move the left foot to the side, small step, turning from the zag to the zig.

Woman Move the right foot to the side, turning from the zag to the zig.

8

COUNT – QUICK

Man Close the right foot to the left foot. End standing on the zig.

Woman Close the left foot to the right foot. End standing on the zig.

The Basic Movement can now be repeated continuously. Curve the Basic Movement comfortably to ease you around corners. This is best done by the man on Step 6, by curving his right foot slightly inwards as he takes this foot back.

Reverse Pivot Turn

Having mastered the Basic Movement, you will soon want to include a new but easy move. The Reverse Pivot Turn is a simple but effective move which will help you to avoid bumping into other dancers ahead of you and one which you will also find helpful for manoeuvring around corners. "Reverse" simply means a turn to the left and does not imply any special type of backward move. Start as for the Basic Movement.

1
COUNT – SLOW

Man Walk forward with the left foot, but check the movement by relaxing the knee. Leave the right foot behind you.

Woman Walk back with the right foot.

2
COUNT – SLOW

Man Rock back smoothly onto your right foot. Keep your right hand firmly in place, to ensure that the woman remains with you.

Woman Rock forward smoothly onto your left foot.

3
COUNT – QUICK

Man Move the left foot to the side, small step, making about a quarter turn (90°) anticlockwise (counterclockwise).

Woman Move the right foot to the side, turning with the man.

4
COUNT – QUICK

Man Close the right foot to the left foot. End standing on the right foot.

Woman Close the left foot to the right foot. End standing on the left foot.

> When using the Reverse Pivot Turn at a corner, you only need to dance the move once to end in your starting position on the new wall. However, when using the Reverse Pivot Turn to avoid other couples, you may repeat the move several times. For example, dancing the Reverse Pivot Turn four times will leave you in exactly the same place as when you started the manoeuvre, allowing other floor traffic ahead of you to clear.

Natural Pivot Turn

In this sense, "natural" just means a turn which goes to the right, that is, clockwise. With a little practice, this move can be added quickly to your repertoire. It is especially useful at corners and for combining with the Reverse Pivot Turn to give the feeling of fluent movement around the floor. Start as before.

Combination
Try dancing the Natural Pivot Turn but along the side of the room. You will then end on a zig, ready to move towards the centre line of the room. Next, dance three Reverse Pivot Turns to leave you back in your starting position.

> In the orientation given below, you will be dancing the Natural Pivot Turn around a corner.

1
COUNT – SLOW

Man Walk forward with the left foot along the zig.

Woman Walk back with the right foot.

2

COUNT – SLOW

Man Walk forward with the right foot, starting to turn right.

Woman Walk back with the left foot, starting to turn right.

3

COUNT – QUICK

Man Move the left foot to the side, turning right to end backing around the room.

Woman Move the right foot to the side, small step, turning right to end facing into the room.

4

COUNT – QUICK

Man Close the right foot to the left foot. End standing on the right foot, backing around the room.

Woman Close the left foot to the right foot. End standing on the left foot, facing into the room.

5

COUNT – SLOW

Man Walk back onto the left foot, turning in the toes to continue turning to the right.

Woman Walk forward onto the right foot, turning to the right.

Notes

Dancers often feel that Steps 5–6 are a little like a rocking movement which helps the turn.

6

COUNT – SLOW

Man Walk forward onto the right foot, continuing to turn to the right to move onto the zig of the new wall.

Woman Walk back onto the left foot, continuing to turn to the right to move onto the zig of the new wall.

7

COUNT – QUICK

Man Move the left foot to the side, continuing to turn right to end on the zag.

Woman Move the right foot to the side, small step, continuing to turn right to end on the zag.

8

COUNT – QUICK

Man Close the right foot to the left foot. End standing on the right foot on the zag.

Woman Close the left foot to the right foot. End standing on the left foot on the zag.

Continue with steps 5–8 of the Basic Movement.

Side-Step Move

Now try a great figure for temporarily slowing down your progress along the room. It is very flexible and can be danced after either Steps 1–2 or Steps 7–8 of the Basic Movement, turning them less so that the man is facing squarely to the wall. The man is standing on his right foot and the woman is standing on her left foot.

1

COUNT – QUICK

Man Left foot to the side.

Woman Right foot to the side.

2

COUNT – QUICK

Man Tap or touch the right foot next to the left foot.

Woman Tap or touch the left foot next to the right foot.

3 ▶

Man Move the right foot to the side.

Woman Move the left foot to the side.

4 ▶

COUNT – QUICK

Man Tap or touch the left foot next to the right foot.

Woman Tap or touch the right foot next to the left foot.

5

COUNT – QUICK

Man Move the left foot to the side.

Woman Move the right foot to the side.

6

COUNT – QUICK

Man Close the right foot to the left foot. End standing on the right foot.

Woman Close the left foot to the right foot. End standing on the left foot.

7

COUNT – QUICK

Man Move the left foot to the side.

Woman Move the right foot to the side.

8

COUNT – QUICK

Man Tap or touch the right foot next to the left foot.

Woman Tap or touch the left foot next to the right foot.

9

COUNT – QUICK

Man Move the right foot to the side.

Woman Move the left foot to the side.

10

COUNT – QUICK

Man Tap or touch the left foot next to the right foot.

Woman Tap or touch the right foot next to the left foot.

> *The man continues with the Basic Movement, but curving the first step onto the zig to lead the woman into the next move and return to the normal alignment.*

Social Dancing: Do's and Don'ts

Courtesy is often seen as an old-fashioned idea, and perhaps for this reason it is an intrinsic element of ballroom dancing – and, after all, politeness and consideration for others are always appreciated. Here are a few broad guidelines which, if followed, will contribute much to enjoying your dance time and to others enjoying theirs.

While it is quite normal in some dance clubs to dance with different partners, it is only fair to dance at least the first and last dance with the partner with whom you arrived. Before asking the woman to dance, it is wise for the man to watch her dancing first with someone else and take note of what she is doing so he won't cause embarrassment by launching into a series of death-defying moves if this is her first dance event. The same applies to a partner whom you have never seen before. Start with basics and build up gradually. If your partner finds something difficult, smile with her and enjoy something she can do. Do not try to show off – no one, least of all a new partner, will appreciate it. If you visit a dance event without a partner, and many do, avoid trying to monopolise one partner. If things work out, you can always make a date to visit again as a couple.

Women should note that it often takes a lot of courage for a man to ask them for a dance. If a man does ask you to dance with him, be flattered and agree to dance. If the partner really is not to your liking, you can make your gentle excuses should he ask you again but, at least, you have done him the courtesy of allowing him a dance with you. If you are shy or a beginner, the man will appreciate your modesty in confiding this to him so that he should not embarrass you by launching into his personal "burn out" programme. Similarly, the man may introduce himself as a beginner when he asks a woman to dance with him.

When taking to the floor, it is important to avoid causing problems for other dancers. Since, in the ballroom dances, the man normally starts a dance facing the wall, it may seem natural for him to walk onto the floor backwards while his attention is focused on his partner. This creates an irritating and unnecessary hazard for other dancers. It is far better to approach the floor and assess the flow of floor traffic before taking up your start position with due consideration for other dancers.

Show consideration for others on the floor and especially so when it is crowded. Avoid dancing moves which take up a lot of room if there is not the room to dance them. If you keep bumping into other dancers, it's time to cool it. In any case, it's much nicer to dance close to your partner when the floor is full – and it is a great opportunity for conversation.

When the dance has finished, thank your partner and leave him or her the option of dancing the next dance with you. It should not be an automatic assumption. If you are leaving the floor, the man should escort his partner at least to the edge of the floor if not back to her seat. When leaving the floor, especially during the course of a dance, the same consideration should be shown. If you are finishing before the music has ended in a travelling dance, you should dance to the edge of the floor and leave the floor at that point.

Under no circumstances should drinks be taken onto the floor. Not only are they likely to be spilled, spoiling the floor, but broken glass on a dance floor is extraordinarily dangerous. If you have to pass the floor on the way from the bar, wait until the dance has finished or find a better spot. Smoking on the dance floor is dangerous and the height of ignorance; an absolute no-no.

Remember that a little consideration can go a long way and is always welcome.

What to Wear

Social dance events happen across a wide spectrum of social levels ad hence degrees of formality or informality. Generally, weekday dances tend to be more casual than Friday or Saturday events. If you are not sure, you should check with the event organizer.

A staggering variety of specially designed dance shoes is now readily available through specialist dancewear suppliers and schools. The designs will be attractive and fashionable but well suited for the purpose, offering foot protection whilst being cool, light and often featuring a silvered-suede non-slip sole. Trainers or sneakers should, however, be avoided, as they not only make the feet hot but also make turning both difficult and dangerous. This can result in sprained or even broken ankles. Your specialist supplier will be pleased to give specific advice appropriate to your chosen dance style.

Right: Clothes that are both stylish and appropriate for your chosen dance style will improve your performance as well as your appearance.

Waltz

The Waltz is one of the favourite standard dances of all time. Whether starting a new relationship with the evening's last dance or celebrating a wedding, the Waltz remains the only dance whose innate romance links it inextricably with life's happier moments.

When we look back at the origins of the Waltz, we discover a dance that has adapted in a remarkable way to changing fashions over the course of its history; a history that has spanned two centuries. The dance that came to symbolize romance started life towards the end of the 18th century as an Austro-German folk dance called the Ländler. It was characterized by the rotary gyrations of men and women dancing together as partners. In the early years of the 19th century, the Waltz took the controversial step of adopting a hold in which the man's right hand was placed around the lady's waist. The great debate concerning the dubious morality of the Waltz continued until the Russian Czar, Alexander, gave the dance the royal seal of approval when he was observed openly dancing and enjoying the Waltz in public. The enormous popularity of the Viennese Waltzes composed and played by the Strauss family though the latter half of the 19th century ensured that, by the century's end, the Waltz had reached the pinnacle of popularity.

By the time of the First World War, a new generation of dancers was looking for a more natural, less stylized way of dancing the Waltz. A revolution in the Waltz style had started to take place with the advent of another dance called the Boston, in which the dancers employed a "modern" closer hold, danced hip to hip and at a more leisurely pace. Although the Boston had virtually disappeared by the outbreak of the War, it was one of the influences on the new-style Waltz.

In 1914 the craze for the Foxtrot spread from America all over Europe, overshadowing the Waltz, which was still perceived to have Germanic associations.

In 1921, with the Waltz all but extinct, *The Dancing Times* called a conference of dance teachers in London to discuss the pressing issues of the day. One of these was the decline in popularity of the Waltz during the war and the confusion arising out of the lack of standard technique. From this conference came the standard "Walk-Side-Close" technique danced today, which characterizes the Modern Waltz. Because these fundamental developments took place in England, the Standard Waltz is sometimes known as the English Waltz. With its newer, more natural feel, the dance soon re-established itself as one of the most popular social dances in the ballroom and became one of the best loved "standard" international dances.

Based on the techniques defined during the 1920s and cultivated through the 1930s, the Waltz has continued to develop through the 20th century giving rise to an astonishing variety of graceful figures and combinations for the enjoyment of those who dance it. I hope you are now about to become one of them.

Basic Floorcraft

While you and other dancers are dancing around the floor, you should be aware of other couples and their likely direction of travel. Knowing how to avoid problems is a great advantage to a dancer and ways of doing this are described in the Floorcraft tips later in the book. There are, however, a few general rules worth mentioning now.

- *It makes sense for more experienced dancers to give way to less experienced couples.*

- *Whoever sees a potential problem should take action to avoid it. This is usually the couple who are further back in the flow of floor traffic.*

- *Never dance across the centre line of the room into the oncoming flow of floor traffic. With a little practice, the ability to avoid dancing into a problem will itself yield satisfaction and enjoyment.*

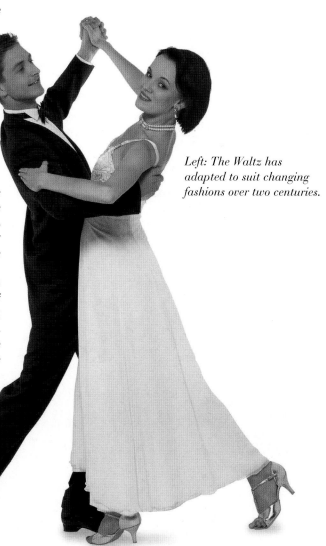

Left: The Waltz has adapted to suit changing fashions over two centuries.

The Basic Waltz

Some schools recommend dancing the Waltz in a straight line around the room. This is not incorrect but, as most dancers zigzag along the floor, the straight-line method continually cuts across the path of other dancers and causes problems for everyone. In addition, the character of the Waltz suggests a dance of elegant turns, so we will start with an internationally recognized method of dancing the Basic Waltz which includes a degree of characteristic turn and which also makes it more interesting and enjoyable.

The Basic Waltz described here consists of four sections of three steps to make a short routine of 12 steps. Each section has a Walk, a Side Step and a Close. Start in the hold described previously with the feet together and standing about 4 feet (1.5 metres) away from the edge of the floor to allow sufficient space to dance into. The man is ready to move forward along a zig and the woman to move backwards along it.

Section 1

1

Man Walk forward with the right foot, curving a little to the right (clockwise).

Woman Walk back with the left foot, curving a little to the right (clockwise).

2

Man Turn from the zig to the zag by moving sideways onto the toes of the left foot.

Woman Turn from the zig to the zag by moving a small step sideways onto the toes of the right foot.

3

Man Now, on the zag, close the right foot to the left foot and lower toe-heel onto the right foot.

Woman Now, on the zag, close the left foot to the right foot and lower toe-heel onto the left foot.

Section 2

4

Man Walk back along the zag onto the left foot, with no turn.

Woman Walk forward along the zag onto the right foot, with no turn.

5

Man Move sideways onto the toes of the right foot, with no turn.

Woman Move sideways onto the toes of the left foot, with no turn.

6

Man Close the left foot to the right foot and lower toe-heel onto the left foot.

Woman Close the right foot to the left foot and lower toe-heel onto the right foot.

Sway

Sway is an important feature of a nice, easy and relaxed style. When reaching with the foot, it is quite natural for the body and head to tilt or sway a little away from the reaching foot, acting as a counterbalance. If small steps are taken, sway will hardly be felt but as you get used to dancing the Waltz and start to move more freely, it will enhance your style if you allow yourself to sway a little away from the reaching foot and towards the closing foot.

FLOW

zag

zig

starting position

Section 3

7

Man Walk back with the right foot, curving a little to the left anticlockwise (counterclockwise).

Woman Walk forward with the left foot, curving a little to the left anticlockwise (counterclockwise).

8

Man Turn from the zag to the zig by moving sideways onto the toes of the left foot.

Woman Turn from the zag to the zig by moving sideways onto the toes of the right foot.

9

Man Now, on the zig, close the right foot to the left foot and lower toe-heel onto the right foot.

Woman Now, on the zig, close the left foot to the right foot and lower toe-heel onto the left foot.

Notes

· Note how the sections start with alternate feet.
· The sections alternate turning moves and straight moves.
· The overall pattern of the Basic Waltz is a zigzag along the floor.
· It is essential to ensure that the second step in each section moves to the side and does not deteriorate into another walking step.
· Do not be tempted to deviate from the pattern described; accuracy is vital.
· Practise your Waltz, trying to relax and settle down to a steady rhythm. You should find that you are staying in a path just over a metre wide.

Bad tracking?

If you find that you are "tracking" towards the centre or towards the wall, you should check that you are making the same amount of turn to the right and to the left in the turning sections (Sections 1 and 3) to keep you on track.

WALL

FLOW

zig   zag

12 11

10

9

8   7

starting position

Section 4

These three steps are only one of four possible examples of a Closed Change Step. A closed change step is any walk-side-close movement without turn. It may move forwards or backwards and may start with either foot.

10

Man Walk forward along the zig onto the left foot, with no turn.

Woman Walk back along the zig onto the right foot, with no turn.

11

Man Move sideways onto the toes of the right foot, with no turn.

Woman Move sideways onto the toes of the left foot, with no turn.

12

Man Close the left foot to the right foot and lower toe-heel onto the left foot.

Woman Close the right foot to the left and lower toe-heel onto the right foot.

You can now repeat the basic 12 steps from the beginning to enjoy waltzing around the room. For the moment, when you reach a corner simply bend the dance around the corner, but make sure that you reorientate yourself as quickly as possible onto the zigs and zags of the new wall. This is best and most comfortably achieved by the man turning to the left more strongly on Step 7.

Natural Turn Around a Corner

Once you have settled down to the regular rhythm and pattern of the Basic Waltz, you will soon want to try a move which will help you turn the corner more fluently and comfortably. In standard dancing, any move which turns clockwise is referred to as a "natural" turn, no matter how unnatural it might feel at first. The Natural Turn comprises two sections of three steps. Each section follows the familiar pattern of walk-side-close. Begin as for the Basic Waltz with the feet together. The man is standing on his left foot and the woman on her right foot, about 4 feet (1.5 metres) from the edge of the floor. The man is ready to move forwards along a zig and the woman to move backwards along it.

Section 1

This section comprises the first three steps of the Basic Waltz but turning them a little more.

1

Man Walk forward with the right foot, curving to the right (clockwise).

Woman Walk back with the left foot, curving to the right (clockwise).

2

Man Continue turning and move sideways onto the toes of the left foot.

Woman Continue turning and then move sideways onto the toes of the right foot (a small step).

3

Man Continue turning to end backing into the corner, facing against the flow. Close the right foot to the left foot and lower onto the right foot. (The wall is now on your left.)

Woman Continue turning to end facing down the room with the flow. Close the left foot to the right foot and lower onto the left foot.

Section 2

Continue turning in the same direction as you cut across the corner to end on the zig at the start of the new wall:

4

Man Continue turning clockwise and walk back with the left foot.

Woman Continue turning clockwise and walk forward with the right foot.

5

Man Continue turning clockwise and move sideways onto the toes of the right foot (a small step).

Woman Continue turning clockwise and move sideways onto the toes of the left foot.

6

Man Continue turning clockwise to end on the zig of the new wall. Close the left foot to the right foot and lower onto the left foot.

Woman Continue turning clockwise to end on the zig of the new wall. Close the right foot to the left foot and lower onto the right foot.

> *You have now successfully turned the corner and are on a zig ready to dance along the new wall using the familiar Basic Waltz.*

Practical tip – Short Steps

On Step 2 for the woman and Step 5 for the man, the dancer should take a slightly shorter step to the side to help their partner turn around them. The person who is dancing backwards into the turn is the one on the "inside" of the turn and should take the shorter steps. This is a very useful tip to remember and try to put into practice throughout the dance.

Rise and Fall

Rise and fall is the elevation and lowering which the dancer feels as he or she moves onto the toes of a foot and then relaxes through the knee, ankle and toes to end on a flat foot. In reality, rise and fall is a by-product of the natural swing of the Waltz. A good swing action is something which dedicated competitors strive to achieve over many years of tough coaching and hard practice. The social dancer can also start to enjoy the gentle rising and falling and add considerably to the feeling of the Waltz by following a few simple guidelines.

Right: A walk forward on count 1 will usually be a normal walk starting with the heel.

Left: A move to the side on count 2 will usually lift onto the toes.

Right: A close on count 3 will usually be accompanied by a lowering (toe to heel) onto the foot that has just moved to close.

Left: On figures with four steps in one bar of music, for example, a Chassé, the dancer will rise more gradually over the first three steps before lowering gently on the fourth (toe to heel action).

• Occasional exceptions to these guidelines are noted in the appropriate figure if considered relevant to the enjoyment of social dancing. Rise and Fall does not occur in the Social Foxtrot or Modern Tango.

Fitting the Basic Waltz into the Room

As you dance the Basic Waltz, you may well find that when you want to dance the Natural Turn at a corner you are not quite in the right position; you could be either ready to dance it too early or not ready until too late. As a general rule, it is much better to dance it early, as the later option could see you disappearing off the edge of the floor. With practice, however, you will be able to gauge your progression around the room so that you arrive near the corner in a perfect position to dance the Natural Turn.

It is often assumed, quite wrongly, that this is achieved by increasing the length of the step. This would in fact make the dancing quite uncomfortable. The answer, though slightly more subtle, is no more difficult. The angle of the turns made during the Basic Waltz can be adjusted to make the dance progress more or progress less along the side of the room. A greater amount of turn will result in more progression and a lesser amount in less progression. An experienced dancer will not worry about reaching the corner in the perfect position until perhaps the last 12 steps of the Basic Waltz, in which the angles can be adjusted to fit the movement into the space available.

Be aware that less experienced dancers often try to dance an extra Basic Waltz when really they ought to have started the Natural Turn or other corner figure. This error often means that the dancer has not planned ahead sufficiently, so it is important to start thinking about the corner as soon as you have danced about two-thirds of the way along the room.

Tighter angle = Less Progression

Wider angle = More Progression

Outside Change

The most useful moves are often the simplest. The Outside Change is a great figure for using as a spacer to extend the Basic Waltz. You can dance the Outside Change immediately after dancing Section 1 of the Basic Waltz. After the Outside Change you will be able to continue by dancing your Basic Waltz again, starting with Section 1 and with the man taking his first step forward with the right foot outside the woman, or by dancing into the Natural Turn around a Corner with the same right foot modification for the man. It can similarly be followed by the Natural Spin Turn which is described later in the book.

2

Man Walk back onto the toes of the right foot, still on the zag.

Woman Walk forward onto the toes of the left foot.

1

Man Walk back onto the left foot, still on the zag.

Woman Walk forward onto the right foot.

3

Man Move sideways onto the left foot, starting to move onto the zig.

Woman Move sideways onto the right foot, starting to move onto the zig.

WALL

zig

1st step of next figure outside partner

zag

starting position

3

2

1

FLOW

It is important to note that on the first step of the figure following the Outside Change, the man will find it more comfortable and natural to dance outside the woman with his right foot: that is, his right foot will move forward between himself and his partner.

The move is completed by continuing into the Basic Waltz or Natural Turn around a Corner.

Outside Change Ending in Promenade Position

This popular and extremely useful floorcraft variation of the Outside Change is used to overtake slower couples ahead or just to enhance your progress around the room. It includes a new move called the Chassé (pronounced sha-say). Begin by dancing Steps 1 and 2 of the Outside Change as before. On Step 2, the man starts to move his head slightly more to the left than usual and the woman starts to move her head to the right. Then continue as follows.

3

Man Take a small step to the side along the room by lowering onto the left foot but pointing the left foot along the zig.

Woman Take a small step to the side along the room by lowering onto the right foot but pointing the right foot along the zag. Move the head over to the right.

In this move, the woman does not turn her body. This results in her ending in a slightly open or "promenade" position on Step 3.

Promenade Position

Promenade Position is a very frequently used position in standard dancing. It simply means that the couple has moved into a position in which the distance between the man's left shoulder and the woman's right shoulder is greater than the distance between the man's right shoulder and woman's left. The couple are therefore slightly open on the man's left and the woman's right side. It is crucial that this very slightly open position is not exaggerated to become an almost side-by-side position. In the Promenade Position, the woman will be looking to the right and the man slightly further to the left than normal. When the man uses his right foot and the woman her left foot to take a step in Promenade Position, it will be taken "through the middle" between the dancers and along the same line. Because of the relative positioning of their bodies, the man's foot will go through first. Such a step should be a short one to avoid distorting the top half of the body.

WALL

FLOW

black lines show body alignment

Chassé from Promenade Position

This frequently used move has four steps. These are fitted into the standard three beats of the Waltz by dancing a special count of 1, 2 &, 3, where the middle counts of 2 & share the second beat of the music. The man dances this move along a single line parallel to the wall but maintaining the zig alignment. The woman dances this move along a single line parallel to the wall but with the head and body gradually turning left to resume the normal position facing the man.

1

Man Move the right foot forward and across yourself along the line.

Woman Move the left foot forward and across yourself along the line, starting to turn to the left.

2

Man Move onto the toes of the left foot, still progressing along the same line.

Woman Move sideways onto the toes of the right foot, along the same line and continuing to turn left.

&

Man Close the right foot to the left foot, still on the toes.

Woman Close the left foot to the right foot, still on the toes, completing the turn to face the man.

3

Man Move sideways, lowering onto the left foot, along the same line to end on the zig.

Woman Move sideways, lowering onto the right foot, along the same line to end on the zig.

> *Continue into the Basic Waltz or Natural Turn around a Corner, remembering that on Step 1, the man will walk forward with the right foot outside.*

Three Walks Curving to the Right

Imagine you are on a zig ready to dance the Basic Waltz but there is another couple ahead of you. You can dance the Three Walks Curving to the Right instead. By the time you have danced this useful figure, the couple who were just ahead of you will probably have moved on, leaving your path clear.

Floorcraft Figures

When you first try out your Basic Waltz at a dance, you will find that one of the man's main preoccupations will be to avoid other dancers on the floor. Sometimes you will find that split-second decisions have to be made to avoid bumping into another couple. It is therefore important that the man leads the woman by making his intentions very clear. He should not and need not physically manoeuvre the woman if he dances his chosen move with clarity. The woman should also try to anticipate possible problems. To stop the man moving backwards into another couple, the woman should squeeze his upper right arm between her left thumb and middle finger as a warning. It is then up to the man to take the avoiding action. It is sensible to choose a figure which will avoid the problem in the simplest way. The easy moves explained here include the Hover Corté, the Whisk and the Checked Natural Turn. These, along with Three Walks Curving to the Right, will help you deal with potential traffic problems.

1

Man Walk forward onto the right foot, starting to curve to the right.

Woman Walk back onto the left foot, starting to curve to the right.

2

Man Move forward onto the toes of the left foot, continuing to curve to the right.

Woman Move back onto the toes of the right foot, continuing to curve to the right.

3

Man Walk forward and slightly across yourself with the right foot, lowering onto the right foot outside the woman and continuing to curve to the right to end on the zag. Turn your body a little further to the right on this step.

Woman Walk back a small step, lowering onto the left foot underneath your body, continuing to curve to the right to end on the zag. Turn your body a little further to the right on this step.

Continue by dancing the Outside Change with an important modification. On Step 1, maintain the turned body position of the end of the Three Walks Curving to the Right. The woman takes her first step of the Outside Change outside the man, that is, between herself and her partner, and will start to turn a little to the left to move in line with the man as she continues into Step 2.

Hover Corté

The Hover Corté (pronounced kor-tay) is a standard figure in the Waltz and can be danced after Step 6 of the Basic Waltz, especially if the way ahead is not clear. Start on a zag, having danced Section 2 of the Basic Waltz. The man is standing on his left foot and the woman on her right. Both have their feet together.

1

Man Walk back onto the right foot, curving a little to the left anticlockwise (counterclockwise).

Woman Walk forward onto the left foot, curving a little to the left anticlockwise (counterclockwise).

2

Man Move sideways onto the toes of the left foot, turning onto the zig.

Woman Turn from the zag to the zig by moving sideways onto the toes of the right foot, allowing the left foot to touch the right foot underneath the body.

3

Man On the zig, lower your body weight sideways onto the right foot.

Woman On the zig, lower your body weight sideways onto the left foot.

Continue with Section 2 of the Basic Waltz. Dance this without any turn so that you remain on the zig. The woman will take Step 1 forward and across herself and outside the man with the right foot. Then start the Basic Waltz from the beginning.

Whisk

The Whisk is a popular and standard move in the Waltz. A good place to dance the Whisk is after Step 9 (Section 3) of the Basic Waltz. Because the Whisk temporarily halts your progress around the room, it is a good delaying move if another couple is in the path ahead. The couple is on a zig with feet together. The man is standing on his right foot and the woman on her left.

1 **Man** Walk forward onto the left foot on the zig.

Woman Walk back onto the right foot on the zig.

2 **Man** Move sideways against the flow onto the toes of the right foot, still on the zig.

Woman Move sideways against the flow onto the toes of the left foot, turning from the zig to the zag.

3 **Man** Lower onto the left foot, crossing it behind the right foot underneath your body and turning your body very slightly to the right.

Woman Lower onto the right foot, crossing it behind the left foot underneath your body.

You are now in a Promenade Position with the woman having opened her right side. Continue with the Chassé from Promenade Position which you danced previously as part of the Outside Change and Chassé from Promenade Position.

Checked Natural Turn with Reverse Pivot

If you are dancing into the Natural Turn around a Corner and you find that the corner is congested with floor traffic immediately ahead of you, you can check the movement into the turn and pivot to the left out of trouble. Start as for the Natural Turn around a Corner.

1 **Man** Walk forward onto the right foot, starting to turn to the right.

Woman Walk back onto the left foot, starting to turn to the right.

2 **Man** Move forward onto the toes of the left foot, turning more strongly to the right but keeping your head looking along the zig. Sway a little to the left.

Woman Move back onto the toes of the right foot, turning more strongly to the right. Sway a little to the right and allow your head to move over to the right.

3 **Man** Curve back, lowering onto the right foot and turning strongly to the left while keeping the left foot in front of the right foot, knees together, to end on the zig of the new wall, or ready to move towards the centre line of the room along the zag.

Woman Move forward, lowering onto the left foot and turning strongly to the left with your knees together. Allow your head to move to the left to resume its normal position. End on the zig of the new wall.

Having negotiated the corner, you can continue to dance into Steps 10–12 (Section 4) of the Basic Waltz or into the Whisk using the zig of the new wall.

Floorcraft Options – a Summary

You now have a number of options to help you cope with floor traffic conditions at each stage of the Basic Waltz and at the corner, if you find the way ahead blocked by other dancers.

As you practise, you will find that you will gradually be able to improve your response time to the floor conditions ahead and will increasingly be able to avoid problems by reading the floor. Of course, you don't have to wait until there is a problem to be avoided before you dance these options. You can dance them to hone your floorcraft skills or just to enjoy them as figures in themselves. Practice not only makes perfect, it makes possible. When you are dancing your repertoire of moves with little effort, it is time to try something a little more challenging.

After Section 1:
Outside Change or Outside Change ending in Promenade Position and Chassé from Promenade Position

After Section 2:
Hover Corté

After Section 3:
Whisk and Chassé from Promenade Position

After Section 4:
Three Walks Curving to the Right and Outside Change

Natural Spin Turn

While it is not a basic figure, the Natural Spin Turn has become the international standard method of turning a corner in the Waltz. As a bonus, the Natural Spin Turn is also the standard corner figure in the Quickstep. The figure starts in the same place as the Natural Turn around a Corner. Think of the Natural Spin Turn as having a total of six steps. You have encountered three of them earlier so, with a little patience, you will soon be able to master this simplified version of the Natural Spin Turn. Start by dancing Steps 1–3 of the Natural Turn around a Corner. The man is facing against the flow with his feet together and standing on his right foot. The woman is facing with the flow with her feet together and standing on her left foot.

4

Man Move back onto the left foot, staying down and turning the left foot inwards to make a strong turn to the right. Keep your knees together. (This will feel awkward but only because you are dancing it step by step. At normal speed, the move will flow much more comfortably.)

Woman Move forward onto the right foot, staying down and turning strongly to the right to end on the zig of the new wall. Keep your knees together.

5

Man Walk forward between the woman's feet onto the right foot on the zig of the new wall. Lift up onto the toes of the right foot and continue turning to the right on the toes of the right foot, keeping the left foot behind.

Woman Move back onto the toes of the left foot on the zig of the new wall, continuing to turn to the right. Bring your right foot back out of the way to touch your left foot.

Style Tip
Some men find it helpful to think of Steps 4–6 as a rock back, a rock forward lifting and a rock back while remembering, of course, to turn. It is a common error for the man to make Step 5 a side step but this must be avoided. It is important for the man to keep his head to the left throughout the figure.

6

Man Relax back onto the left foot away from the corner, having turned onto the zag of the new wall.

Woman Move forward, lowering onto the right foot on the zag of the new wall.

Floorcraft Tips
If you find the corner blocked as you start the Natural Spin Turn, you can stop the figure by dancing the Checked Natural Turn with Reverse Pivot described earlier.

Note that the feet do not close. Continue by dancing straight into Section 3 of the Basic Waltz.

Hover Telemark

The Hover Telemark is a classic figure which is not only extremely useful but also has a superb look and feel and is not difficult to lead. The description of the moves needs to be carefully followed before success will be achieved. Do not confuse the name of this move with the Hover Corté described earlier. Dance this figure after Section 3 of the Basic Waltz. You will now be on a zig with your feet together. The man is standing on his right foot and the woman on her left.

1

Man Walk forward onto the left foot along the zig but turning your body to the left so that you are almost walking across yourself. Relax the knees and look along the zig.

Woman Walk backward onto the right foot along the zig but turning your body to the left so that you are almost walking across yourself. Relax the knees and turn your head well to the left as you feel the clear lead of this figure.

2

Man Move forward along the zig onto the toes of the right foot, turning your body to the right so that it comes square with the feet.

Woman Move back along the zig onto the toes of the left foot, turning your body to the right so that it comes square with the feet. Move your head gradually over to the right to end facing the man.

3

Man Take a small step to the side along the room by lowering onto the left foot and pointing it along the zig in a Promenade Position.

Woman Take a small step to the side along the room by lowering onto the right foot and pointing it along the zag. Move your head over to the right to finish in a Promenade Position.

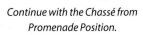

Continue with the Chassé from Promenade Position.

Open Telemark Group

Now that you have had some practice at combining the figures you have learned and have become familiar with various features of the Waltz, including the Promenade Position, you will certainly want to try a new combination as this move is introduced. Take care and consider the other dancers, as this combination moves you across the flow towards the centre line of the room. First, though, you will need to position yourself ready to dance the Open Telemark.

Section 1

Dance the Natural Spin Turn as you would at a corner and using the same amount of turn, but this time dance it along the side of the room. When you have danced a complete turn (360°), you will end on the zig against the flow.

Section 2

Dance Section 3 of the Basic Waltz to end facing towards the centre line of the room but on the zag. You will have turned a quarter turn (90°) to the left. You are now ready to experience the elegance of the Open Telemark.

1

Man Walk forward onto the left foot along the zag towards the centre line, starting to turn to the left.

Woman Walk back onto the right foot along the zag towards the centre line, starting to turn to the left.

2

Man Move forward onto the toes of the right foot, still along the zag towards the centre line and continuing to turn to the left. End with the right foot to the side, backing the zig.

Woman Close the left foot to the right foot with the left heel in contact with the floor. Continue turning to the left on the heel of the right foot and move your head gradually over to the right as you rise onto the toes of the left foot.

3

Man Continue turning on the right foot and take a small step to the side, lowering onto the left foot and pointing it along the zig in Promenade Position.

Woman Continue turning on the left foot and take a small step to the side, lowering onto the right foot and pointing it along the room in Promenade Position. Your head is now to the right.

Continue with the Chassé from Promenade Position or the Hairpin from Promenade Position.

Hairpin from Promenade Position

The Outside Change, the Whisk, the Hover Telemark and the Open Telemark can or do all end in Promenade Position and would normally be followed by the Chassé from Promenade Position. However, as the route ahead may sometimes be blocked, it is useful to have an alternative course available to you. Here is a superb figure which always looks more difficult than it is, giving professional polish to the Waltz of even moderate dancers. Start by dancing any of the figures listed above, ending in Promenade Position.

1

Man Move the right foot forward and across yourself along the line.

Woman Move the left foot forward and across yourself along the line.

Style Tip
The man dances Steps 1–2 along a single line parallel to the wall but maintaining the zig alignment. The woman dances Steps 1–2 along a single line parallel to the wall.

2

Man Move onto the toes of the left foot, pointing them along the zig. Close the woman to your right side by turning your body slightly to the left.

Woman Move sideways onto the toes of the right foot, along the same line but turning strongly to the left to close your right side to the man. Your head resumes its normal left position.

3

Man On the left foot, sway and turn strongly to the right onto the zag. Take a small step forward, lowering onto the right foot outside the woman. Turn your body a little further to the right as you take this step and move your head to the right to look at the woman. Note that the body turn occurs before the step.

Woman Take a small step back, under your body, lowering onto the left foot and turning strongly to the right to end on the zag. Turn your body a little further to the right as you take this step.

> *Note the strong sway to the right for the man and to the left for the woman on Step 3. Continue into the Outside Change.*

Hairpin from Step 6 of the Basic Waltz

The Hairpin does not have to be danced from the Promenade Position. It can also be started from Step 6 of the Basic Waltz, in which case it is modified as follows. Use it in any situation where the way ahead is blocked and you wish to delay your progress around the room.

1 ▶

Man Walk back onto the right foot along the zag.

Woman Walk forward onto the left foot along the zag.

2

Man Move sideways onto the toes of the left foot.

Woman Take a small step sideways onto the toes of the right foot.

◀ 3

Man On the left foot, sway and turn a little to the right, still on the zag. Take a small step forward and across yourself, lowering onto the right foot outside the woman. Turn your body a little further to the right as you take this step and move your head to the right to look at the woman.

Woman Take a small step back under your body, lowering onto the left foot and turning a little to the right. Turn your body a little further to the right as you take this step.

> *Continue as from the Three Walks Curving to the Right.*

Hover from Promenade Position

It is always good practice and style to have a floorcraft figure up your sleeve which you can dance if the way ahead is obstructed. This one can be danced after the Whisk, the Outside Change Ending in Promenade Position, the Open Telemark or the Hover Telemark. Steps 2 and 3 are similar to the Hover Corté but the entry is from a Promenade Position.

1

Man Walk forward and across yourself onto the right foot, in Promenade Position.

Woman Walk forward and across yourself onto the left foot, in Promenade Position.

2

Man Take a small step forward onto the toes of the left foot, turning to the left. Lead the "hover" by swaying to the right.

Woman Walk forward onto the toes of the right foot, turning to the left to end facing the man with your feet side by side but apart. Sway to the left and turn your head to the left.

3

Man Move back against the flow line lowering onto the right foot to end facing the zig.

Woman Move forward against the flow line lowering onto the left foot.

Continue with one of the figures suggested for following the Progressive Chassé to the Right. You may even dance into the Open Impetus Turn from this position. Remember that the next step for the woman will be a forward walk with her right foot outside the man.

Three Walks Curving to the Left

To add interest and flexibility to your Waltz, we will now introduce a move which turns to the left. First dance Section 1 and 2 of the Open Telemark Group. The man is now on the zag facing towards the centre line of the room and the woman is opposite. The couple have their feet together. The man is standing on his right foot and the woman her left foot. Although this move ends with the man facing against the flow, as you dance this figure, be careful not to actually move against the flow.

1

Man Walk forward with the left foot, curving to the left.

Woman Walk back with the right foot, curving to the left.

2

Man Walk forward onto the toes of the right foot, still curving and swaying to the left.

Woman Walk back onto the toes of the left foot, still curving and swaying to the left.

3

Man Brushing the left foot past the right foot, walk forward, lowering onto the left foot and continuing to curve.

Woman Brushing the right foot past the left foot, walk back, lowering onto the right foot underneath the body and continuing to curve.

The figure ends with the man facing against the flow and the woman facing with the flow. By making small adjustments to the amount of turn, you can now dance the Hairpin (as if after step 6 of the Basic Waltz) or the Hover Corté both ending with the man on the zig facing towards the wall. A spectacular continuing move is the Oversway.

Oversway

This classic figure has a number of forms and styles; in this version, the couple come to a temporary halt as the man leads the woman into a turn enhanced by a slightly exaggerated sway. Since the turn is done in place, this move is also useful as a very classy floorcraft figure. Start by dancing the Three Walks Curving to the Left. The man is now facing against the flow, standing on his left foot with feet together. The woman is facing with the flow, standing on her right foot. The Oversway is danced along a line parallel to the wall.

1

Man Walk back along the line onto the right foot.

Woman Walk forward onto the left foot.

2

Man Walk back along the line onto the left foot, relaxing the knee then, on the left foot, start to swivel to the left, with a slight sway to the left, and lead the woman as if you are moving her into Promenade Position.

Woman Walk forward onto the ball of the right foot as if ready to pass the man, leading with your right side, and flex the right knee, leaving the left foot extended behind. On the right foot, swivel to the left with a slight sway to the right. End with your head to the right.

3

Man Still on the left foot, with the knee flexed and increasing the sway to the left slightly, continue to swivel to the left to end facing the wall with the right foot extended to the side but without any weight on it.

Woman Still on the right foot, with the knee flexed and increasing the sway to the right slightly, continue to swivel to the left to end backing the wall with the left foot extended to the side but without any weight on it.

4

Man Still on the left foot with the left knee flexed and the right foot extended to the side, continue to swivel onto the zig, changing the sway from left to right and bringing your left side back a little and pushing forward through the hips.

Woman Still on the right foot with the knee flexed and the left foot extended to the side, continue to swivel onto the zig, changing the sway from right to left and allowing your head to return to the left. The sway to the left should be slightly exaggerated by turning the body a little more to the left.

5

Man Close the right foot to the left foot, then lift onto the toes of the right foot and neutralize the sway, leading the woman into Promenade Position.

Woman Close the left foot to the right foot, then lift onto the toes of the left foot and neutralize the sway as you return your head to the right to end in Promenade Position.

6

Man Take a small step sideways along the room, lowering onto the left foot in Promenade Position.

Woman Take a small step sideways along the room, lowering onto the right foot in Promenade Position.

The best exit is now a Chassé from Promenade Position, though any of the exits suggested for the Promenade Position can be selected.

Swing

A good swing epitomizes the action used by expert dancers of the Waltz. While in the early stages of getting to grips with the Waltz, you will not have much time to think about developing a good action, but sooner or later you will want to enhance your enjoyment and improve your style with a little bit of swing. If you were to suspend a pendulum from the ceiling, then pull it back and release it to fall by the force of gravity, it would travel in an arc along a straight line. You can begin to use such a natural swing in your waltz. In most of the figures in standard dancing, swing acts on alternate sides of the body in each bar of music or set of three steps. Swing can be applied to any figure and here the Natural Turn is used as an example.

Left: On Step 1, the man walks forward with his right foot along the zig.

Left: As the man turns to the right on Step 2, swing will act on his left side, causing him to rise and helping to propel his left side towards the wall faster than his right side, which has become the centre of the turn.

Right: On Step 3, the swing naturally continues upwards, taking the man's left side with it and causing him to turn and continue rising with the swing's momentum. When the dancer is turning, the swing action will also cause him or her to incline the body towards the centre of the turn – this inclination is called "sway".

Right: Since swing occurs in a straight line, the feet also use that straight line. Steps 1–3 of the Natural Turn are all taken on the same line (in this example, on the zig), irrespective of the turn and where the feet happen to be facing. On Steps 4–6, each step will be taken on the same floorboard or line parallel with the wall, while the swing will act on the man's right side.

Style Tip

When dancing with a swing action, Step 2, which is usually a side step, carries the powerful swing momentum and will therefore be longer than Steps 1 or 3.

Swing is responsible for maintaining a proportional amount of turn, alignment, rise and fall, footwork, sway and length of step in many Waltz figures. Swing also leads to a less energetic and more economical way of moving. It is an important ingredient of good dancing and one which your local coach or dance school can help you develop further.

Quickstep

Right: With its lively tempo, the Quickstep is now one of the most popular ballroom dances.

The Quickstep is one of the two most popular of the International Standard ballroom dances, along with the Waltz. Allegedly, the dance owes its existence to the American comedian Harry Fox, who worked the burlesque theatres of the USA just prior to the First World War. At that time, regulations prohibited semi-clad female performers from moving on stage, and required them to remain in fixed poses in "artistic" tableaux. Fox hit upon the idea of performing a little dance movement around the statically posed women in between jokes. The popular music industry, known as Tin Pan Alley, was soon promoting the music and steps of the "Foxtrot".

The Foxtrot consisted of a slow walk taking two beats of music and a series of quick steps, or trots, each taking a single beat of music. Initially, it relied heavily upon moves from other dances such as the One-step and the Rag, but teachers soon created new figures to meet the demand. By 1915, the Foxtrot reached England and it had soared to new heights of popular acclaim. At this point, the Foxtrot was danced at a tempo of about 32 bars per minute, but in 1916 dancers started to adapt the dance to slower music with a more gliding feel. To differentiate it from the usual, quicker Foxtrot, this slower Foxtrot was initially called the Saunter, and it was this dance which later laid the basis for the Slow Foxtrot.

By the end of the First World War, jazz was coming into its own, expressing the post-war mood of liberation. In the 1920s, the tempo of life quickened, as did the pace of the jazzed-up Foxtrot. By the mid-1920s, dance bands frequently played the Foxtrot at a cracking 50 bars per minute – the Quick Foxtrot. Then, in 1925, the Charleston appeared. While extremely popular as a fad dance, the Charleston lacked long-term

potential. However, in 1927 it was combined with the Quick Foxtrot to result in a dance with the tediously lengthy name of the Q.T.F.T. & C. – the Quick Time Fox Trot and Charleston. The Charleston fell into decline, but its influence lived on in the Q.T.F.T. & C., now renamed the Quickstep.

Through the 1930s and 1940s, the Quickstep's lively character embraced the Big Band Swing sounds. In the 1950s, 1960s and beyond, there were always plenty of foot-tapping tunes and romantic up-tempo melodies for which the Quickstep was the natural dance choice. While the tempo has gradually come down from the athletic 54–56 bars per minute of 1929 to a pleasant 48–50 bars per minute for social dancing in the 1990s, the Quickstep has lost nothing of its lust for life.

At its most advanced, the Quickstep is a combination of body swing movements and syncopated hops, danced at an impressive speed. At its most social, the dance offers a repeatable basic pattern which everyone can enjoy. We hope that you and your partner will embrace the rhythm and swing of what has become the classic Quickstep.

Music

Quickstep music is organized with four beats to each bar of music. The first and third beats are both accentuated by the musicians but the first beat is stronger. It is on the first strong beat that you will take your first step of the dance. You will become familiar with counting the steps of the moves in "Quicks" and "Slows". A "Quick" equates to a single beat of music while a "Slow" equates to two beats. Most of the basic moves in the Quickstep start with a "Slow" count followed by two "Quick" counts. Some, like the Quarter Turn to the Right, are then completed with a further "Slow" count, while others, such as the Natural Turn, have a different rhythm. Note that, because both the first and third beats are accentuated, you will not necessarily complete a move in a single bar of music. The Quarter Turn to the Right with a count of "Slow-Quick-Quick-Slow" will take 1½ bars of music, while a Natural Turn with a count of "Slow-Quick-Quick-Slow-Slow-Slow" will take 2½ bars of music. You need not be consciously aware of this while you are dancing; it is sufficient to be aware of the "Slows" and "Quicks" of the steps you are dancing.

Musically, the time signature of the Quickstep is 4/4 with a tempo currently recommended internationally at 50 bars per minute, although, for social dancing, Quicksteps can be enjoyed at tempos ranging from 48 to 52 bars per minute. This tempo is a little faster than a brisk walking pace but can seem very fast indeed to start with. However, as you grow more familiar with the Quickstep and remember to take small steps as you dance, the momentum of the moves themselves will help you to cope with the tempo.

Basic Quickstep

The Basic Quickstep described here consists of two sections: a forwards half and a backwards half. Both halves travel along the room in an overall anticlockwise (counterclockwise) direction, with the flow. The side-close-side movement in Steps 2–4 of both halves of the Basic Quickstep is known as a "chassé" (pronounced "sha-say"). Start in the hold described in the introduction to International Standard Partner Dancing, with the feet together and standing about 4 ½ feet (1.5 metres) away from the edge of the floor to allow sufficient space to dance into. The man is ready to move forward along a zig and the woman to move backwards along it.

Forward Half
Quarter Turn to the Right

1
COUNT – SLOW

Man Walk forward with the right foot along the zig, starting to turn to the right.

Woman Walk back with the left foot along the zig, starting to turn to the right.

2
COUNT – QUICK

Man Move sideways onto the toes of the left foot, travelling along the room but facing the wall.

Woman Move sideways onto the toes of the right foot, travelling along the room but facing the centre line.

3
COUNT – QUICK

Man Close the toes of the right foot to the toes of the left foot, continuing to turn to end on the zag, backing the centre line of the room.

Woman Close the toes of the left foot to the toes of the right foot, continuing to turn to end on the zag.

4
COUNT – SLOW

Man Walk back along the zag towards the centre line, lowering toe-heel onto the left foot.

Woman Walk forward along the zag towards the centre line, lowering toe-heel onto the right foot.

WALL

FLOW

zag

starting position

Zig

Backward Half
Progressive Chassé

1

COUNT – SLOW

Man Walk back along the zag with the right foot, moving towards the centre line and starting to turn to the left.

Woman Walk forward along the zag with the left foot, moving towards the centre line and starting to turn to the left.

Practical Tip

As you try out the Basic Quickstep for the first time, avoid taking big steps. It looks smarter and is more comfortable to keep your steps small and neat.

2

COUNT – QUICK

Man Move sideways onto the toes of the left foot, travelling along the room and pointing the left foot along the zig.

Woman Move sideways onto the toes of the right foot, travelling along the room and turning a little to the left to end with your back square to the wall.

3

COUNT – QUICK

Man Close the toes of the right foot to toes of the left foot. End facing the zig.

Woman Close the toes of the left foot to the toes of the right foot, continuing to turn to the left to end backing along a zig.

4

COUNT – SLOW

Man Move sideways, lowering toe-heel onto the left foot to end pointing along the zig.

Woman Move sideways, lowering toe-heel onto the right foot.

You can now repeat the Basic Quickstep with one important difference. On each subsequent Step 1 of the Basic Quickstep or other following move, the man will walk forward with his right foot outside the woman's right side. The woman's steps remain the same.

Rise and Fall

Rise and fall is the elevation and lowering which the dancer feels as he or she moves onto the toes of a foot and then relaxes through the knee, ankle and toes to end on a flat foot. Rise and fall will therefore take the dancer both above and below normal height. In reality, rise and fall is a by-product of the natural swing of the Quickstep, giving the dance its speed and flow which have ensured its liveliness and continuing appeal. A good swing action is something which dedicated competitors strive to achieve over many years of rigorous coaching and strenuous practice. Social dancers can also introduce rise and fall and enjoy the improved feeling and appearance of their dance by following a few simple guidelines.

Left: A walk forward on Step 1 will usually be a normal walk, staying down, though starting to rise at the very end of the step as the body weight rolls over the toes.

Left: On the last step of the bar, whether that is Step 3 or 4, the dancer will usually lower toe-heel onto the flat foot.

Right: A move to the side on Step 2 will usually lift onto the toes.
- *Generally, the dancers will walk, either staying down or lowering on a slow count.*
- *Most "Quick" counts are danced on the toes.*

Right: On figures with four steps in one bar of music, for example, a Chassé, the dancer will rise more gradually over the first three steps before lowering gently on the fourth using a toe-heel action.

Natural Turn Around a Corner

In all the standard dances, including the Quickstep, special figures have been devised to help dancers turn around a corner. Here is one of the easier ones, which will help you to flow easily around the corner and leave you in exactly the right position to continue dancing the Basic Quickstep along the new wall. Start having danced the Basic Quickstep. The man is standing on his left foot ready to move forward towards the wall along a zig and the woman is standing on her right foot ready to move backwards along the zig. You can, of course, start the dance with the Natural Turn at a corner if that is where you take to the floor. This option is depicted here. However, if you are dancing the move after a Basic Quickstep then remember that the man's first step will be outside his partner.

Natural Turn

1
COUNT – SLOW

Man Walk forward with the right foot along the zig starting to turn to the right.

Woman Walk back along the zig with the left foot, starting to turn to the right.

2
COUNT – QUICK

Man Move sideways along the zig onto the toes of the left foot, continuing to turn to the right.

Woman Move sideways along the zig onto the toes of the right foot, continuing to turn to the right.

3

COUNT – QUICK

Man Close the toes of the right foot to the toes of the left foot and lower onto the right foot, turning to face against the flow.

Woman Close the toes of the left foot to the toes of the right foot and lower onto the left foot, turning to face with the flow.

Around a corner

4

COUNT – SLOW

Man Walk back with the left foot, continuing to turn to the right and releasing the right toes from the floor but keeping the heel in contact with it.

Woman Walk forward with the right foot, continuing to turn to the right.

5

COUNT – SLOW

Man Pull the right foot back with the heel in contact with the floor, then slide the foot around, continuing to turn to end facing along the zig of the new wall, with the right foot to the side of the left foot and with feet apart.

Woman Move sideways onto the left foot, continuing to turn to the right to face the wall.

6

COUNT – SLOW

Man Walk forward with the left foot along the zig of the new wall.

Woman Walk back with the right foot, continuing to turn to the right to move back along the zig of the new wall.

WALL

NEW WALL

FLOW

zig of new wall

starting position

zig

Natural Spin Turn

You are already familiar with the Natural Spin Turn as the standard method of turning corners in the Waltz. It is also the standard recognized way of turning corners in the Quickstep. In Quickstep, the Natural Spin Turn can be danced after the Basic Quickstep followed by Steps 1-3 of the Natural Turn around a corner remembering that the man takes the first step outside partner. The Natural Spin Turn in Quickstep has a different timing to the Waltz.

1–3

COUNT – SLOW, QUICK, QUICK

Dance steps 1–3 of the Natural Turn around a Corner.

Dance Tip
When dancing this figure, it is important for the man to keep his head to the left throughout the figure.

4

COUNT – SLOW

Man Move back onto the left foot, turning it inwards to make a strong turn to the right. Keep your knees together. (This will feel awkward at first but only because you are dancing it step by step. At normal speed, the move will flow more comfortably.)

Woman Move forward onto the right foot, turning strongly to the right to end with your back to the zig of the new wall. Keep your knees together.

5

COUNT – SLOW

Man Walk forward between the woman's feet onto the right foot on the zig of the new wall and lift up onto the toes of the right foot. Continue turning to the right on the toes of the right foot, keeping the left foot behind.

Woman Move back onto the toes of the left foot on the zig of the new wall, continuing to turn to the right. Bring the right foot back out of the way to touch the left foot.

6

COUNT – SLOW

Man Relax back onto the left foot away from the corner, having turned onto the zag of the new wall.

Woman Move forward, towards the centre-line lowering onto the right foot on the zag of the new wall.

Continue by dancing straight into the backward half of the Basic Quickstep – the Progressive Chassé.

Practical Tip
Some men find it helpful to think of Steps 4–6 as a rock back, a rock forward lifting and a rock back, while remembering to turn. It is a common error for the man to make Step 5 a side step (shown right).

Lock Step

You can now dance a continuous Basic Quickstep with either the Natural Turn or Natural Spin Turn at the corners. The Lock Step will complete your repertoire of International Standard Basic Quickstep figures. The name is a little misleading as the feet cross only loosely and do not actually "lock". The steps are the same for both the man and the woman. While the man dances the Forward Lock Step, the woman dances the Backward Lock Step, and vice versa. The man dances the Forward Lock Step and the woman the Backward Lock Step after the Basic Quickstep as a useful spacer for improving positioning prior to dancing one of the corner figures. It can also be inserted between two groups of the Basic Quickstep. As you dance the Lock Step, imagine a line parallel to the wall and dance along it.

Forward Lock Step

Start facing the zig, with feet apart and standing on the left foot. Throughout this move, remain facing along the zig but travelling along the line parallel to the wall.

1

COUNT – SLOW

Walk forward with the right foot, outside your partner's right side onto the line parallel with the wall.

2

COUNT – QUICK

Walk forward onto the toes of the left foot along the line.

3

COUNT – QUICK

Still on the toes of the left foot, cross the right foot loosely behind the left foot.

4

COUNT – SLOW

Walk forward along the line, lowering onto the left foot.

Double Lock Step

For a classy combination of the Lock Step which will add sparkle to your Quickstep, Steps 2 and 3 can be repeated before continuing into Step 4. This is called the Double Lock Step.

WALL

FLOW

Backward Lock Step

Start backing the zig, with feet apart and standing on the right foot. Throughout this move, remain backing along the zig but travelling along the line parallel to the wall.

1

COUNT – SLOW

Walk back with the left foot onto the line parallel with the wall.

2

COUNT – QUICK

Walk back onto the toes of the right foot along the line.

3

COUNT – QUICK

Still on the toes of the right foot, cross the left foot loosely in front of the right foot.

4

COUNT – SLOW

Walk back along the line, lowering onto the right foot.

Fitting the Basic Quickstep into the Room

As you dance the Basic Quickstep, you may well find that when you want to dance the Natural Turn or the Natural Spin Turn at a corner you are not quite in the right position. As a general rule, it is much better to dance the corner figure early, as the later option could see you disappearing off the edge of the floor. With practice, however, there will no longer be a danger of this as you will be able to gauge your progression around the room so that you arrive near the corner in a perfect position to dance around it.

In the Quickstep, the length of the steps should never be increased to the point where the figures and movement become distorted. It is much better to adjust the angles of the zigs and zags during the Basic Quickstep. A greater amount of turn will result in more progression along the floor and a lesser amount in less progression. In addition, figures such as the Lock Step can be used to extend a Basic Quickstep by half as much again to help put you in the right position. Be aware that less experienced dancers often try to dance an extra Basic Quickstep when really they ought to have started the corner figure. This error often results from the dancer not having planned ahead sufficiently, so it is important to start thinking about the corner as soon as you have danced about halfway along the room.

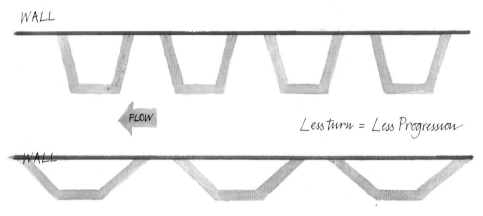

WALL

FLOW

Less turn = Less Progression

WALL

More Turn = More Progression

Natural Hairpin and Running Finish

Imagine you are on a zig ready to dance the Basic Quickstep or the Lock Step and the way ahead of you is not clear. Now is the time to dance the Natural Hairpin and conclude it with a very stylish flowing movement called the Running Finish, which can also be used later with other figures.

Natural Hairpin

1

COUNT – SLOW

Man Walk forward with the right foot, curving it outside the woman's right side onto the zig, and start turning to the right.

Woman Walk back with the left foot, starting to curve to the right.

2

COUNT – QUICK

Man Move forward onto the toes of the left foot, continuing to curve strongly to the right.

Woman Move back onto the toes of the right foot, continuing to curve strongly to the right.

Style Tip
To help your turn, see how the man will bank or sway to the right and the woman to the left on Steps 2–3.

3

COUNT – QUICK

Man Walk forward, lowering onto the right foot, slightly across yourself and outside the woman, continuing to curve to the right to end facing almost against the flow.

Woman Take a small step back, lowering onto the left foot underneath your body and continuing to curve strongly to the right to end facing almost with the flow.

WALL

FLOW

centre line

starting position

zig

Timing Tip
Until you get the hang of this figure, Steps 2 and 3 can be danced as slows.

Running Finish

The Running Finish can also be danced after Steps 1–3 of the Natural Turn or the Natural Spin Turn. In this case, Step 2 for the woman will be taken in line with the man. At a corner, simply go with the flow and bend the Running Finish around it.

1

COUNT – SLOW

Man Move back along the zig under your body, starting to turn to the right.

Woman Walk forward with the right foot, outside the man's right side and turning to the right along the zig.

2

COUNT – QUICK

Man Move sideways onto the toes of the right foot facing the centre line and, still turning to the right, sway to the left.

Woman Move sideways onto the toes of the left foot facing the wall and, still turning to the right, sway to the right.

3

COUNT – QUICK

Man Swing your left side forward to face with the flow, swaying to the left, and move forward, lowering onto the left foot.

Woman Swing your right side back to face against the flow, swaying to the right, and take a short step back, lowering onto the right foot.

Continue by dancing the Basic Quickstep with the man moving his right foot forward outside the woman on the first step and turning a little more than usual to resume the normal orientation. Alternatively, you can dance the Lock Step. For added style, try combining the Natural Hairpin, the Lock Step (Backward for the man, Forward for the woman) and the Running Finish, before resuming with either the Forward Lock Step (for the man) or the Basic Quickstep.

Outside Change

This is another very simple figure but one which has a nice feel to it and which will help add variety to your increasing repertoire of Quickstep moves. It is a good floorcraft move, enabling you to overtake slower couples immediately ahead. In this move, the woman does not turn her body. This results in her ending in a slightly open or "promenade" position on Step 3. You can insert it into your programme after Steps 1–3 of the Natural Turn or the Natural Spin Turn, having reduced the amount of turn ("underturned") a little so that the man ends on a zag facing the wall. The man is standing on his right foot and the woman on her left. Both have their feet together.

1
COUNT – SLOW

Man Walk back with the left foot along the zag.

Woman Walk forward with the right foot.

2
COUNT – QUICK

Man Walk back onto the toes of the right foot, still on the zag, starting to turn to the left.

Woman Walk forward onto the toes of the left foot.

3
COUNT – QUICK

Man Take a small step to the side along the room by lowering onto the left foot to end facing the wall in Promenade Position, with the left foot pointing along the zig.

Woman Take a small step to the side along the room by lowering onto the right foot, pointing it down the room and moving your head to the right to end in Promenade Position.

Continue with the Chassé from Promenade Position.

Chassé from Promenade Position

A Chassé is simply a side-close-side movement, and you have already danced this in the Basic Quickstep. Here, the Chassé is danced from the Promenade Position following the Outside Change. The dancers move along a line parallel to the wall but maintaining their zig alignment. In addition, the woman gradually moves her head to the left as she resumes her normal position facing the man.

1
COUNT – SLOW

Man Take a short step forward and across yourself with the right foot, along the line.

Woman Walk forward and across yourself with the left foot, along the line and starting to turn to the left.

2
COUNT – QUICK

Man Move onto the toes of the left foot, still progressing along the same line.

Woman Move sideways onto the toes of the right foot, along the same line and continuing to turn to the left.

3

COUNT – QUICK

Man Close the toes of the right foot to the toes of the left foot.

Woman Close the toes of the left foot to the toes of the right foot, completing the turn to face the man.

4

COUNT – SLOW

Man Move sideways, lowering onto the left foot along the same line to end on the zig.

Woman Move sideways, lowering onto the right foot along the same line to end on the zig.

WALL

FLOW

Continue into the Basic Quickstep, the Natural Turn around a Corner or the Natural Spin Turn, remembering that on Step 1 of the next figure, the man will walk forward with the right foot outside the woman.

Hover Corté

You can dance the Hover Corté immediately after the Forward Half of the Basic Quickstep (the Quarter Turn to the Right) if your path into the Backward Half (the Progressive Chassé) is blocked. The man is standing on his left foot and the woman on her right, with feet apart.

1

COUNT – SLOW

Man Walk back along the zag with the right foot, starting to turn to the left.

Woman Walk forward along the zag with the left foot, starting to turn to the left.

2

COUNT – SLOW

Man Move sideways onto the toes of the left foot, turning onto the zig and swaying to the right.

Woman Move sideways onto the toes of the right foot, turning onto the zig and swaying to the left.

3

COUNT – SLOW

Man On the zig, lower your body weight sideways onto the right foot.

Woman On the zig, lower your body weight sideways onto the left foot.

Having successfully avoided the problem on the dance floor, continue as follows on the next page.

4

COUNT – SLOW

Man Walk back with the left foot, moving temporarily against the flow.

Woman Walk forward with the right foot, outside the man's right side and moving temporarily against the flow.

5

COUNT – QUICK

Man Move sideways onto the toes of the right foot, swaying to the left.

Woman Move sideways onto the toes of the left foot, swaying to the right.

6

COUNT – QUICK

Man Standing on the toes, close the left foot to the right foot and lower onto the left foot, still swaying to the left. End on the zig.

Woman Standing on the toes, close the right foot to the left foot and lower onto the right foot, still swaying to the right. End on the zig.

> *Continue into the Basic Quickstep, the Natural Turn, the Natural Spin Turn or the Natural Hairpin, remembering that on Step 1 of the next figure, the man will walk forward with the right foot outside the woman.*

Natural Turn with Hesitation

This is a useful variation of the Natural Turn, which can be danced near the beginning or middle of a wall and which combines well with other figures described later in the book. Start by dancing the first three steps of the Natural Turn Around a Corner.

1–3

Dance steps 1–3 of the Natural Turn Around a Corner.

4

COUNT – SLOW

Man Walk back with the left foot, continuing to turn to the right and releasing the right toes from the floor but keeping the heel in contact with it.

Woman Walk forward with the right foot, continuing to turn to the right.

5

COUNT – SLOW

Man Pull the right foot back with the heel in contact with the floor, then slide the foot around to end to the side of the left foot, with feet apart. Continue turning to the right to end facing along the zag towards the centre line.

Woman Move sideways onto the left foot, staying down with flexed knees and continuing to turn to the right to end on the zag facing the wall.

6

COUNT – SLOW

Man Slide the left foot to close to the right foot but remain standing on the right foot.

Woman Slide the right foot to close to the left foot but remain standing on the left foot.

Continue with the Progressive Chassé to the Right, the Chassé Reverse Turn or the Quick Open Reverse Turn, which are described later.

Sway

Sway is rather like the banking of a motorcyclist travelling around a bend in the road. It is an important feature of a nice, easy and relaxed style. When dancing a section of Quickstep which has only three steps in the bar, for example, a walk-side-close movement during a turn, it is quite natural for the body and head to tilt or sway a little away from the reaching foot to act as a counter-balance. Natural sway will occur on Steps 2–3 of the Natural Turn in the Swing Dances, to the right for the man and to the left for the woman. Sway is therefore an essential feature of balancing comfortably as you dance.

Chassé Reverse Turn

This is a short but useful figure which follows the Natural Turn with Hesitation described earlier. In dancing terminology, "reverse" simply refers to a turn to the left. It does not mean that the figure moves backwards. The man is standing on his right foot and the woman on her left with the feet almost closed. The man is facing the centre line along the zag and the woman is backing the centre line along the zag.

1

COUNT – SLOW

Man Walk forward with the left foot, along the zag towards the centre line, starting to turn to the left.

Woman Walk back with the right foot, along the zag towards the centre line, starting to turn to the left.

2

COUNT – QUICK

Man Move sideways onto the toes of the right foot, continuing to turn to the left. Sway to the left.

Woman Move sideways onto the toes of the left foot, continuing to turn to the left. Sway to the right.

3

COUNT – QUICK

Man Close the left foot to the right foot and lower onto the left foot. Continue to sway to the left and turn to end facing against the flow.

Woman Close the right foot to the left foot and lower onto the right foot. Continue to sway to the right and turn to end facing with the flow.

Continue with the Progressive Chassé (the Backward Half of the Basic Quickstep) but turning it a little more than usual to resume its normal orientation.

Style Tip
The man will curve his left foot into this move to help lead the turn while the woman will ensure that she takes a shorter step on Step 2 to help the man move around her. The important thing is to keep the flow moving through the turn and allow it to run out into the following chassé.

Progressive Chassé to the Right

Following the Natural Turn with Hesitation, this figure can move you quickly and easily along the floor with the flow around the room. The Chassé, as usual, is danced along an imaginary line parallel to the wall.

1

COUNT – SLOW
Man Walk forward onto the left foot, starting to turn to the left.

Woman Walk back onto the right foot, starting to turn to the left.

2

COUNT – QUICK
Man Move sideways along the line onto the toes of the right foot, continuing to turn to the left to end with your back square to the wall.

Woman Move sideways along the line onto the toes of the left foot, continuing to turn to face the wall.

3

COUNT – QUICK

Man Close the toes of the left foot to the toes of the right foot, continuing to turn to the left to end backing along the zig.

Woman Close the toes of the right foot to the toes of the left foot, continuing to turn to the left to end facing along the zig.

4

COUNT – SLOW

Man Move sideways, still along the line, lowering onto the right foot.

Woman Move sideways, still along the line, lowering onto the left foot.

You can now continue with a super-smooth ending: either dance the Backward Lock Step followed by the Running Finish or go straight into the Running Finish.

V-6 Combination

When a figure combination becomes popular, it often becomes a set piece in the dance. The V-6 combines the Backward Lock Step with a modified Outside Change. As the name suggests, the figure makes a "V" pattern, which makes it ideal to dance along the short side of the floor.

The Entry

Dance the Natural Spin Turn Around a Corner at the end of a long side and finish it with the man backing the new centre line along a zag. Alternatively, dance Steps 1–3 of the Natural Spin Turn, starting on the short side (after a Natural Turn Around a Corner) and underturning the move to 90° to end backing the new centre line along a zag.

Backward Lock Step

If you danced the Natural Spin Turn as the entry, now dance Steps 2–4 of the Lock Step (Backward for the man and Forward for the woman), moving towards the centre line of the short side of the floor. If the alternative entry of Steps 1–3 of the Natural Turn has been used, then dance Steps 1–4 of the Lock Step (Backward for the man and Forward for the woman), with the woman taking her first step in line with the man.

Outside Change

The Outside Change is now modified to fit the different context in which it is danced.

1

COUNT – SLOW

Man Walk back with the left foot underneath your body, along the zag.

Woman Walk forward with the right foot outside the man's right side.

2

COUNT – QUICK

Man Walk back onto the toes of the right foot, still on the zag and starting to turn to the left.

Woman Walk forward onto the toes of the left foot, starting to turn to the left.

3

COUNT – QUICK

Man Take a small step to the side along the room by lowering onto the left foot to end facing the wall, with the left foot pointing along the zig.

Woman Take a small step to the side along the room by lowering onto the right foot to end backing the wall.

Lock Step Exit

The best exit to this combination is for the man to dance the Forward Lock Step and the woman to dance the Backward Lock Step. The angle at the point of the "V" may be adjusted so that the V-6 can be fitted exactly into the short side of many ballrooms. If you find that this is the case, you can return to your programme by dancing into one of the corner figures, such as the Natural Spin Turn, remembering that the first step of the following figure for the man will be outside his partner. Otherwise, continue into the Basic Quickstep or a "natural" figure.

Summary of Counts for the V-6 Combination

Natural Spin Turn	Slow, Quick, Quick, Slow, Slow, Slow
Steps 2–4 of the Backward Lock Step (man) and Forward Lock Step (woman)	Quick, Quick, Slow
Modified Outside Change	Slow, Quick, Quick
Forward Lock Step (man) and Backward Lock Step (woman)	Slow, Quick, Quick, Slow

If the alternative entry is used, the count will be:

Steps 1–3 of the Natural Spin Turn	Slow, Quick, Quick
Steps 1–4 of the Lock Step	Slow, Quick, Quick, Slow

Tipple Chassé Around a Corner

Now that you are building up a repertoire of useful and enjoyable figures, you can combine parts of the moves you already know with a new element in a popular and attractive group – the Tipple Chassé. This is a very flexible figure and, in the first combination, you can use it around a corner. Remember to allow sufficient room ahead of you to dance the figure. For the entry, start by dancing Steps 1-3 of the Natural Turn Around a Corner or the Natural Spin Turn.

Entry

The man is now facing against the flow with his feet together and standing on his right foot. The woman is facing with the flow with her feet together and standing on her left foot.

1

COUNT – SLOW

Man Walk back with the left foot, starting to turn to the right.

Woman Walk forward with the right foot, starting to turn to the right.

Style Tip
The man should dance this section taking small steps.

2

COUNT – QUICK

Man Move sideways onto the toes of the right foot, completing a quarter (90°) turn to the right to face with the flow along the new wall. Sway to the right and look past the woman's left shoulder.

Woman Move sideways onto the toes of the left foot, completing a quarter (90°) turn to the right to face against the flow along the new wall and swaying to the left.

Variation
When you have practised the standard Tipple Chassé, you can develop it further by introducing the Backward Lock Step for the man and the Forward Lock Step for the woman between the Entry and the Tipple Chassé. The woman must make some modifications to ensure that the move goes smoothly:

• take Step 1 of the Forward Lock Step in line with the man.

• take Step 1 of the Tipple Chassé outside the man's right side. The count for this Lock Step will be the usual slow, quick, quick, slow.

3

COUNT – QUICK

Man Close the toes of the left foot to the toes of the right foot, still swaying to the right.

Woman Close the toes of the right foot to the toes of the left foot, still swaying to the left.

4

COUNT – SLOW

Man Move sideways onto the toes of the right foot, swaying to the right and turning onto the zig of the new wall.

Woman Move sideways onto the toes of the left foot, swaying to the left and turning onto the zig of the new wall.

Continue along the zig of the new wall by dancing Steps 2–4 of the Forward Lock Step for the man and the Backward Lock Step for the woman. The man will move his left side forward and the woman her right side back as they move into the Lock Step.

Tipple Chassé along the Room

In this combination, the Tipple Chassé is used in a different position.
This time, you will be dancing it along the side of the room.

Entry

Dance the Progressive Chassé to the Right, followed by the Backward Lock Step for the man and the Forward Lock Step for the woman, along the zig.

1

COUNT – SLOW

Man Walk back with the left foot, starting to turn to the right.

Woman Walk forward with the right foot, outside the man's right side, starting to turn to the right.

2

COUNT – QUICK

Man Move sideways onto the toes of the right foot, turning to the right. Sway to the right and look past the woman's left shoulder.

Woman Move sideways onto the toes of the left foot, turning to the right and swaying to the left.

Style Tip
The man should dance this section taking small steps.

3

COUNT – QUICK

Man Close the toes of the left foot to the toes of the right foot, still swaying and looking to the right.

Woman Close the toes of the right foot to the toes of the left foot, still swaying to the left.

4

COUNT – SLOW

Man Move sideways onto the toes of the right foot, swaying to the right and turning onto the zig.

Woman Move sideways onto the toes of the left foot, swaying to the left and turning onto the zig.

Continue by dancing Steps 2–4 of the Forward Lock Step for the man and the Backward Lock Step for the woman. The man will move his left side forward and the woman her right side back as they move into the Lock Step.

Modern Tango

The **"Modern"** in Modern Tango differentiates it from the original and authentic style of Argentine Tango. By the early 1930s, the Tango had been so changed from the original style in order to conform with the conventions of the ballroom, that it had developed into a completely different and quite separate dance. The Modern Tango established itself as one of the standard dances of the ballroom and as a compulsory dance for Standard Championships. The hard, arrogant style of the Tango in competition dancing belies its essentially romantic nature when danced in a social setting. For competitive dancing, the infamous and affected Tango head-flicks have become the established style, but these are not necessary just to enjoy dancing the Modern Tango for the fun and pleasure it can bring.

The Modern Tango does, however, use a very different technique to the other Standard dances, and we must first explore some of these differences. They exist because, unlike the other Standard dances, the Tango is not a "swing dance". The power and impetus come from the legs rather than from the body swing of the Waltz, Quickstep or Slow Foxtrot. There is therefore no sway, rise or fall, and the Tango is danced flat and into the floor. This actually makes it easier to learn for first-time dancers. The hold is also different.

Music Suggestions
"La Cumparsita" must be the world's best-known and best-loved Tango. The James Last version of "Adios Pampa Mia", written by two of the masters of Tango composition, is my personal favourite, though it does need slowing down slightly for dancing. Klaus Hallen's arrangement of "Verano Porteño" is an excellent version of an authentic Argentinian Tango. Many Tango compilation albums exist, but be careful to choose one which specifies that it is for dancing rather than for listening. Those recorded by the Japanese orchestra of Hisao Sudou are very good and are readily available from specialist dealers worldwide.

The Tango Hold & Feet Position

Take up a normal ballroom hold. Now, allowing the feet to swivel on the spot, twist the body and feet a little to the left. The result of twisting the body and legs to the left will mean that the right foot will be slightly behind the left foot, so that the inside edge of the ball of the right foot nestles against the instep of the left foot. Both knees will be flexed. The man's right hand will now be a little further around the woman's back – the man lowers his right hand a little. The woman places her left hand *under* the man's upper right arm, ensuring that her fingers are straight. The man's lower left and the woman's lower right arm are flattened slightly towards the floor.

The Hold & Feet Position seen from behind.

The Hold & Feet Position seen in front.

The Tango Walks

The method of walking in Tango has become an important and integral feature of the dance. Due to the slightly twisted starting position:

- any walk forward with the left foot will be taken slightly across the body.

- any walk back with the left foot will be taken with the left side of the body moving with the moving foot.

- any walk forward with the right foot will be taken with the right side of the body advancing with the moving foot.

- any walk back with the right foot will be taken slightly across the body.

This means that a series of forward walks would quite naturally curve a little to the left. If the walks are made to go in a straight line, the effect and feel will be of a slight crabbing action. This may seem strange at first but it will soon become an integral part of the dance for you.

Forward walk with the left foot.

Backward walk with the left foot.

Forward walk with the right foot.

Backward walk with the right foot.

Timing and Rhythm

The time signature of the Modern Tango is officially 2/4 but many Tangos are also arranged to a 4/4 time signature. This need not concern the social dancer, who can recognize a Tango by its march-like rhythm. The tempo or speed of the dance is normally 32–33 bars per minute.

The basic rhythm of the Modern Tango is Quick-Quick-Slow, but many moves either incorporate or are often preceded by two preparatory Slow walks.

The Tango Action

The "action" merely describes the type or style of movement used. In Tango, it is important to "place" the feet. That is to say that the feet are picked up and placed gently but firmly in position. They are not slid along the floor and they should never be stamped down. When releasing a foot from the floor, the heel should be released first and then the rest of the foot peeled off. All forward walks will be with a heel. In side movements, the inside edge of the foot will usually contact the floor first and then the body weight will be rolled on to the foot. When closing, the foot will be flat.

Much is made of the Tango "staccato" action. It is true that experienced dancers do enhance the appearance and style of the Tango by a sharp action, but the ways of doing this are often misunderstood by less-experienced dancers. The staccato action is a result of a sharp movement which stops suddenly and clearly. The effect, though, is greater than reality, because the abrupt and clear stopping of the movement causes the spectator's eye to continue following the track of the movement for a fraction of a second. This is interpreted by the brain with an over-compensation for what has actually happened. Thus, the staccato action is a clever visual illusion and, like the head-flicks, should be explored under the guidance of an experienced instructor. Dancers who don't develop this skill under expert guidance tend to produce an exaggerated effect which is less than flattering to their dancing.

Leading

As in the other Standard Partner dances, the man establishes a frame with his hold. If the man's arms are held in place and are not allowed to move independently of the body, the woman will be held in the frame and will have little option but to follow the man's intentions. While both dancers' movements are strong, the man must never push or pull the woman into a move or position.

The Rock Turn

To start your Tango, we will use a gentle basic move which includes two easy turns. The couple start on the zig as normal, having first adopted the special Tango hold. The man is standing, feet together, on the right foot and the woman, feet together, on her left foot. Be sure to use the Tango Walk technique and the appropriate action.

1

COUNT – SLOW

Man Walk forward with the left foot along the zig.

Woman Walk back with the right foot.

2

COUNT – SLOW

Man Walk forward with the right foot along the zig.

Woman Walk back with the left foot.

3

COUNT – QUICK

Man Rock back onto the left foot.

Woman Rock forward on to the right foot.

4

COUNT – QUICK

Man Rock forward onto the right foot.

Woman Rock back onto the left foot.

Between Steps 2–5, gradually turn right to end on the zag.

5

COUNT – SLOW

Man Walk back onto the left foot.

Woman Walk forward onto the right foot.

6

COUNT – QUICK

Man Walk back onto the right foot starting to turn left.

Woman Walk forward onto the left foot, starting to turn left.

7

COUNT – QUICK

Man Left foot to the side onto the zig.

Woman Right foot to the side onto the zig.

8

COUNT – SLOW

Man Close the right foot to the left foot, to end standing on the right foot on the zig.

Woman Close the left foot to the right foot, to end standing on the left foot on the zig.

You can now repeat the move as often as you like as you progress around the room. At a corner, dance the same move but miss out the turn over Steps 2–5 and you will end on the zig of the new wall. When you feel comfortable with the Rock Turn, it's time to try out the Progressive Link.

The Progressive Link and Closed Promenade

This is one of the classic moves of the Modern Tango. It is the Progressive Link which, for competitors, incorporates the famous head-flick, but here, we can enjoy a less ostentatious version. Start in the same position as for the Rock Turn.

The Progressive Link

1

COUNT – QUICK

Man Walk forward with the left foot along the zig.

Woman Walk back onto the right foot along the zig and, on the right foot, swivel a little to the right, turning the head to look along the room.

2

COUNT – QUICK

Man Step sideways onto the right foot, turning the body to face the wall. End in Promenade Position.

Woman Step sideways and back onto the left foot to end in Promenade Position, with the head to the right.

Style Point

To enhance the feel and appearance of the Progressive Link, the man may suggest added emphasis to the move by looking across the woman's left shoulder on Step 1 before returning his head to the left to look along the room on Step 2. When this decoration is exaggerated and emphasized, it results in the head-flick previously mentioned.

> *Promenade Position is explained fully in the Waltz section.*

The Closed Promenade

It is conventional in Tango terminology, but confusing for students, to name Modern Tango moves in the reverse order to the sequence in which they happen. A Closed Promenade can therefore be more appropriately explained as a Promenade movement with a Close. Here's how to do it. The dancers have completed the Progressive Link by achieving a Promenade Position. In the Closed Promenade, the dancers move from that Promenade Position back to a closed or normal position.

1

COUNT – SLOW

Man Left foot to the side in Promenade Position.

Woman Right foot to the side in Promenade Position.

2

COUNT – QUICK

Man Right foot forward and across, along the room, still in Promenade Position.

Woman Left foot forward and across, along the room, still in Promenade Position, but starting to turn left.

> *During this move, the woman gradually turns to the left to end facing the man. The woman gradually returns her head to left over the move.*

3

COUNT – QUICK

Man Move the left foot to the side on to the zig.

Woman Turning left to face the man, move the right foot along the room.

4

COUNT – SLOW

Man Close the right foot to the left foot on the zig.

Woman Facing the man, close the left foot to the right foot.

Topical Tip
It is helpful for the dancers to think of themselves travelling along a set of tramlines. The man travels along one and the woman along the other. Each takes his or her own steps precisely on that tramline.

> *The Progressive Link and Closed Promenade can now be alternated with the Rock Turn. If, however, you find you are gradually dancing closer to the wall, you can remedy this problem by changing the angle of the entry into the Rock Turn to be more shallow, and by increasing its first turn more to the right. It's fun building up your experience by experimenting.*

The Combination Reverse Turn

We now need to put together a short amalgamation of moves which, individually, would consist of the progressive side step, right foot walk and reverse turn, woman outside, closed finish. This combination will take you away from the wall and towards the centre line of the room as you progress along it, making a turn to the left. After the previous figures, this will add balance to the overall look and feel of your Tango. Let's now break down the combination into its constituent parts and build them up together. The dancers start in the normal position.

The Progressive Side Step

In this move, you will turn a quarter turn (90°) to the left over its three steps. Starting on the zig, you will therefore end on the zag, facing the centre line of the room.

1

COUNT – QUICK

Man Walk forward with the left foot, starting to curve to the left.

Woman Walk back with the left foot, starting to curve to the left.

2

COUNT – QUICK

Man Move the right foot to the side and slightly back, continuing the curve to the left.

Woman Move the right foot to the side and slightly forward, continuing the curve to the left.

3

COUNT – SLOW

Man Walk forward with the left foot onto the zag, towards the centre line of the room.

Woman Walk back with the right foot onto the zag, towards the centre line of the room.

The Reverse Turn

The dancers now need to dance a single walk – the man with the right foot and the woman with her left foot along the zag, towards the centre line in preparation for the Reverse Turn.

1
COUNT – QUICK

Man Walk forward onto the left foot, starting to turn left.

Woman Walk back onto the right foot, starting to turn left.

2
COUNT – QUICK

Man Move the right foot to the side, turning left to end backing along the zig.

Woman Move the left foot to the side turning left.

3
COUNT – SLOW

Man Move left foot back, underneath the body.

Woman Walk forward onto the right foot, along the room, outside the man.

4
COUNT – QUICK

Man Walk back on the right foot along the room.

Woman Walk forward on the left foot, along the room, in line with the man.

5
COUNT – QUICK

Man Turn onto the zig, left foot to the side.

Woman Turn onto the zig, right foot to the side.

6
COUNT – SLOW

Man Close the right foot to the left foot on the zig.

Woman Close the left foot to the right foot on the zig.

WALL

CENTRE LINE

REVERSE TURN

FLOW

PROGRESSIVE SIDE STEP

zig

zag

zig

The Reverse Turn Variation

When basic figures or moves are modified, they are called variations. Here is a variation of the Reverse Turn which will add extra verve to the basic figure. The variation comes in the second part of the Reverse Turn, so you can dance Steps 1–4 as normal.

5
COUNT – QUICK
Man Left foot to the side facing the wall.

Woman Right foot to the side facing the centre line.

6
COUNT – &
Man Close the right foot to the left foot.

Woman Close the left foot to the right foot.

7
COUNT – SLOW
Man Tap or touch the left foot to the side moving into Promenade Position, looking along the room.

Woman Tap or touch the right foot to the side moving into Promenade Position, looking along the room.

> *Note that the count on Steps 5–6 is split so that the two steps are danced in just one beat of music. Continue from the Promenade Position with the Closed Promenade that you danced earlier, following the Progressive Link.*

The Brush Tap

You have already used the Progressive Side Step and a Walk to manoeuvre from the zig on to the zag, ready to dance the Reverse Turn. The nature of that move makes it inherently cautious. Here is an alternative which is much bolder and more confident – the Brush Tap. Start as you would for the Progressive Side Step. Start on the zig in the starting position. The man is standing on his right foot and the woman on her left foot.

1
COUNT – QUICK
Man Walk forward onto the left foot, starting to curve to the left.

Woman Walk back on to the right foot, starting to curve to the left.

2
COUNT – QUICK
Man Walk forward and sideways, onto the right foot, continuing to curve to the left to end on the zag, ready to move forward towards the centre line.

Woman Walk back and side onto the left foot, continuing to curve to the left to end backing along the zag, towards the centre line.

3
COUNT – &

Man Bring the left foot to touch the right foot.

Woman Bring the right foot to touch the left foot.

4
COUNT – SLOW

Man Touch the left foot to the side, without weight.

Woman Touch the right foot to the side, without weight.

> *The best effect is achieved by keeping the head and upper body still during the Brush Tap on Steps 3–4. It is a mistake to try and embellish the move with any head movements because they detract from the sharpness of movement in the feet, making the move look untidy. Continue with two Tango Walks into the Reverse Turn, or with the Reverse Turn Variation.*

Cornering

Care should be taken to choose an appropriate way of turning around corners in the Modern Tango. A Reverse Turn should never be used, as it not only distorts the shape of the figure but is extremely uncomfortable for the woman. The Rock Turn is an excellent figure to use, when no turn is made over Steps 2–5. This will be comfortable for both the man and the woman. The Progressive Side Step, followed by a right-foot Walk for the man and a

left-foot Walk for the woman to a count of "Slow" is another useful way of turning a corner. This can then be followed at the start of the new side by the Rock Turn, the Progressive Link or by another Progressive Side Step as part of the Combination Reverse Turn. Another useful figure to choose at a corner is the Four Step.

The Four Step at a Corner

This is a neat and compact move which is excellent to use at a corner. Start near to the corner on a zig. The man is standing on his right foot, feet together, and the woman on her left foot, feet together.

1
COUNT – QUICK

Man Walk forward with the left foot, starting to turn left.

Woman Walk back with the right foot, starting to turn left.

2
COUNT – QUICK

Man Move to the side and slightly back on to the right foot, completing a quarter turn to the left, to end on the zig of the new wall.

Woman Move to the side and slightly forward onto the left foot, along the zag.

Style Tip
Advanced dancers will sharpen up the Four Step by splitting the beat on Step 1, to dance the Walk on the first part and the turn on the second part of the beat.

3

COUNT – QUICK

Man Walk back underneath the body onto the left foot.

Woman Walk forward with the right foot outside the man's right side.

4

COUNT – QUICK

Man Close the right foot to the left foot and end in Promenade Position with the head to the right.

Woman Swivelling a quarter turn (90°) to right on the right foot, close the left foot to the right foot, moving the head to the right, to end in Promenade Position.

Continue along the new wall by dancing the Closed Promenade.

The Four Step Along the Side of the Room

The Four Step's versatility also enables it to be danced along the side of the room where it has become a standard figure. Start in the normal position on a zig.

1

COUNT – QUICK

Man Walk forward with the left foot along the zig.

Woman Walk back with the right foot along the zig.

2

COUNT – QUICK

Man Move to the side and slightly back onto the right foot along the zag towards the wall.

Woman Move to the side and slightly forward onto the left foot along the zag.

3

COUNT – QUICK

Man Walk back underneath the body onto the left foot.

Woman Walk forward with the right foot outside the man's right side.

4

COUNT – QUICK

Man Close the right foot to the left foot and end in Promenade Position.

Woman Swivelling a quarter turn (90°) to the right on the right foot, close the left foot to the right foot, moving the head to right to end in Promenade Position.

You are now ready to move from Promenade Position along the zag towards the centre line. You can achieve this with the Closed Promenade, ending with the man facing along the zag towards the centre line of the room. The man should then take a small step on step 3 and follow with the Reverse Turn. Alternatively, try the smart Promenade Link.

The Promenade Link

The Promenade Link should not be confused with the Progressive Link, which is a completely different figure. We shall use the Promenade Link as a snappy way of moving from Promenade Position to a normal position, having danced the Four Step along the side of the room. Start in Promenade Position on the zag, ready to move towards the centre line of the room. The man is on his right foot and the woman on her left foot.

1

COUNT – SLOW

Man Move sideways along the zag onto the left foot, still in Promenade Position.

Woman Move sideways along the zag onto the right foot, still in Promenade Position.

2

COUNT – QUICK

Man Walk forward and across onto the right foot, starting to turn left.

Woman Walk forward and across on to the left foot, starting to turn left and closing the body towards the man.

3

COUNT – QUICK

Man Touch the left foot to the side without weight, knees together, turning to end facing along the zag towards the centre line.

Woman Touch the right foot to the side without weight, knees together, turning to end facing the man with the head to the left.

Continue either straight into the Reverse Turn, or two Walks into the Reverse Turn or Reverse Turn Variation.

The Outside Swivel

You now have, in your repertoire, a variety of ways of dancing into the Reverse Turn and Reverse Turn Variation. Let us now explore a classy option that you can enjoy instead of the Reverse Turn.

1
COUNT – QUICK

Man Walk forward onto the left foot, starting to turn left.

Woman Walk back onto the right foot, starting to turn left.

2
COUNT – QUICK

Man Right foot to the side, turning left to end backing along the zig.

Woman Move sideways on to the left foot, still turning left.

◀ 3 ▶
COUNT – SLOW

Man Move back onto the left foot underneath the body along the zag and, swivelling on the left foot, slide the right foot left until it's pointing along the zig towards the wall.

Woman Walk forward onto the right foot outside the man's right side. Then, bring the left foot to the right foot and swivel a quarter turn to the right on the right foot.

> *Conclude the move by dancing Steps 2–3 of the Promenade Link so that the man ends on the zig, facing the wall. It is important for the woman not to take too big a walk on Step 3 and for the couple to keep the move reasonably compact. A nice figure to follow the Outside Swivel is the Progressive Link and Closed Promenade. At a corner, dance either the Four Step or the Rock Turn as described earlier.*

The Five Step

The Five Step is one of the most flexible, compact and useful figures in the Modern Tango and is full of character and style. One of the most popular places to include the Five Step is instead of the Reverse Turn or Outside Swivel. Start as for a Reverse Turn or Outside Swivel.

1
COUNT – QUICK

Man Walk forward onto the left foot, starting to turn left.

Woman Walk back onto the right foot, starting to turn left.

2
COUNT – QUICK

Man Move the right foot to the side, turning left to end backing along the zig.

Woman Move sideways onto the left foot, still turning left.

3
COUNT – QUICK

Man Move back onto the left foot along the zag, leading the woman to dance outside your right side.

Woman Walk forward onto the right foot outside the man's right side, along the zag.

4

COUNT – QUICK

Man Move back onto the right foot along the zag, leading the woman to dance in line. Turn the body slightly to the left and turn the head to look to the right over the woman's left shoulder.

Woman Walk forward on to the left foot in line with the man, still along the zag.

5

COUNT – SLOW

Man Touch the left foot to the side, without weight, leading the woman into Promenade Position, and turning the head smartly to the left to look along the zig.

Woman Touch the right foot to the side without weight, moving into Promenade Position and turning the head smartly to the right to look along the zig.

Continue with the Promenade Link ending with the man facing along the zig towards the wall. The Five Step can also be substituted for the Four Step by reducing the amount of turn to correspond with the pattern of the Four Step.

The Four Step Photo Figure

This is a fabulous figure and one which develops the Four Step into a photo opportunity. The distinctive "X"-line, which is the highlight of the move, is one which top dancers often use for competitions and which photographers love to capture, as it just exudes the look, feel and character of Modern Tango. Dance the Four Step along the side of the room as previously described.

The "X"-line

The couple achieve the "X"-line on Step 5. It is so called because the lines through the bodies and legs form an "X".

5

COUNT – SLOW

Man Flex the right knee and sharply move the left foot out to point to the side, without weight, at right angles to the zag line, and leading the woman to turn slightly to her right.

Woman Flex the left knee and sharply move the right foot out to point back and to the side, without weight, at right angles to the zag line and turning slightly to the right.

6

COUNT – SLOW

Man Retaining a flexed right knee, move the extended left foot back in a circular movement "Rondé". When it is behind the right foot, move back onto the left foot, a small step, along the zag towards the wall.

Woman Retaining a flexed left knee, move the extended right foot back in a circular movement "Rondé", and when it is behind the left foot, move back onto the right foot, a small step, along the zag towards the wall.

7

COUNT – &

Man Close the right foot sharply to the left foot, turning square to the woman.

Woman Close the left foot sharply to the right foot, turning square to the man.

8

COUNT – SLOW

Man Touch the left foot to the side, without weight, and turn the head to the left in Promenade Position.

Woman Touch the right foot to the side, without weight, and turn the head to the right in Promenade Position.

> *Continue with Closed Promenade, moving along the zag towards the centre line or with the Promenade Link.*

Special Effects

Great special effects can be used in the Modern Tango to create the atmosphere of the dance. Perhaps surprisingly, with a little bit of know-how, many of these effects are quite easy to put into practice.

Stillness is the Essence of Tango

If other floor traffic is blocking your route, stop and remain perfectly still. Do not attempt to move again until your path is clear. Dancers often find it difficult just to stop and remain still but, in the original Argentine Tango, pauses formed an integral and essential part of the dance, and these can be used very effectively in the Modern Tango too.

Moving into Promenade Position with Panache

Imagine you are in your normal starting position and another couple is obstructing your intended path towards the wall. You can wait, or you can move sharply into Promenade Position and then progress down the room.

1

COUNT – &

Man Extend and point the left foot forward and slightly across, leg straight, without weight, and looking to the right over the woman's left shoulder.

Woman Extend and point the right foot back and slightly beneath the body, leg straight, without weight. Turn the head a little more to the left than normal.

2

COUNT – SLOW

Man Bring the left foot sharply back to touch to the side, without weight, in Promenade Position.

Woman Bring the right foot sharply forward to touch to the side, without weight, in Promenade Position and turn the head sharply to the right.

The Promenade Chassé

The Promenade Chassé is a very effective way of moving along the room in Promenade Position while creating a special effect. Start and finish in Promenade Position and keep the knees flexed throughout.

1

COUNT – QUICK

Man Move sideways onto the left foot in Promenade Position.

Woman Move sideways onto the right foot in Promenade Position.

2

COUNT – QUICK

Man Close the right foot to the left foot in Promenade Position.

Woman Close the left foot to the right foot in Promenade Position.

3

COUNT – QUICK

Man Repeat Steps 1–2.

Woman Repeat Steps 1–2.

4

COUNT – SLOW

Man Touch the left foot to the side without weight, and in Promenade Position.

Woman Touch the right foot to the side, without weight, and in Promenade Position.

Polishing up a Pause in Promenade

When in Promenade Position and the way ahead is not clear, you can make a feature of the delay as follows.

1

COUNT – SLOW

Man Move back underneath the body onto the left foot.

Woman Move back underneath the body onto the right foot.

2

COUNT – &

Man Close the right foot sharply to the left foot, turning square to the woman.

Woman Close the left foot sharply to the right foot, turning square to the man.

3

COUNT – SLOW

Man Touch the left foot to the side, without weight, and turn the head to the left in Promenade Position.

Woman Touch the right foot to the side, without weight, and turn the head to the right in Promenade Position.

Slow Foxtrot

The Slow Foxtrot, as its name suggests, is the slower version of the Foxtrot. The quicker version of the Foxtrot evolved into the Quickstep, and the background to both dances is described in the Quickstep chapter. The Slow Foxtrot is a beautiful, romantic dance which has become the classic swing dance of the ballroom and the dance to which ballroom dancers most aspire. However, the simple, graceful lines of the Slow Foxtrot belie the technical understanding, dance experience and physical skill required to produce them. It is customary and advisable, therefore, for dancers discovering the Slow Foxtrot to have previously mastered the basics of the Waltz and Quickstep. Practice not only makes perfect, it makes possible and, with repeated practice, the sheer delight of this dance's understated and sophisticated elegance comes ever closer.

Timing and Rhythm

The Slow Foxtrot has a gentle tempo of 30 bars per minute, a time signature of 4/4 and a steady rhythm of Slow-Quick-Quick, where a Slow equals two beats and a Quick equals one.

Music Suggestions

Slow Foxtrot engenders the best of swing, like "On the Sunny Side of the Street", and contemporary favourites like "This Business of Love" from the hit movie The Mask. *Romantic ballads such as "Nice 'n' Easy" by Frank Sinatra and Hugo Strasser's superb version of "Autumn Leaves" "Der Schleier Viel" are also classic Slow Foxtrots. Whatever your musical taste, you will be able to indulge it by consulting your specialist dance music supplier.*

The Slow Foxtrot is undoubtedly more of a challenging dance than the other Standard Partner dances. However, with a growing understanding, a lot of application and not a little practice, you will be surprised at how much you can achieve and how great the rewards are. Contact your local qualified dance teacher for further help in enjoying the Slow Foxtrot.

A Short Programme

The Slow Foxtrot, unlike the Waltz, Quickstep and Social Foxtrot, does not have a simple, enjoyable, repeatable basic move, so we must first build up a short programme of 12 steps, consisting of the Feather Finish, the Three Step and the Impetus Turn.

The Feather Finish

It may seem odd to start a dance with a Feather Finish, but this is simply the ending of another figure which we shall encounter later. Take up the standard hold. The man is standing on his left foot, feet together on the zig and the woman on her right foot, feet together.

Sway

Sway is the natural inclination of the body as a result of swing. It helps to give a nice, easy, relaxed style to the movement. When reaching to make a step on one foot, the body will naturally tend to incline in order to counterbalance itself. In Slow Foxtrot, the swing will generally alternate from one side of the body to the other over three steps. At the changeover point from one swing to another, there will be no sway. The sway pattern of Slow Foxtrot will therefore generally be straight-right-right, straight-left-left and will then repeat. Exceptions to the sway pattern will occur on certain types of turns, such as the Impetus Turn.

1

COUNT – SLOW

Man Walk back onto the right foot and extend the left foot to rest sideways along the zag.

Woman Walk forward onto the left foot and extend the right foot to rest sideways along the zag.

> *Man's Sway – straight-right-right*
> *Woman's Sway – straight-left-left*

2

COUNT – QUICK

Man Transfer the body weight onto the toes of the left foot.

Woman Transfer the body weight onto the right foot.

3

COUNT – QUICK

Man Lower the body weight, toe-heel, stepping forward with the right foot outside the woman's right side and onto the zig.

Woman Walk back onto the left foot along the zig.

Continue with the Three Step, Reverse Wave or Hover Telemark.

Style Tip

It is important for the woman that, on each backward step in Slow Foxtrot, the toe of the front foot is released from the floor first.

The Three Step

1

COUNT – SLOW

Man Walk forward onto the left foot in-line with the woman and swing the right foot forward along the zig.

Woman Walk back onto the left foot, releasing the toe of the front foot.

Man's Sway – straight-left-left
Woman's Sway – straight-right-right

2

COUNT – QUICK

Man Transfer the body weight forward onto the right foot and lift from the heel onto the toes of the right foot.

Woman Walk back onto the right foot, releasing the toe of the front foot.

3

COUNT – QUICK

Man Lower the body weight stepping forward, toe-heel, onto the left foot along the zig.

Woman Walk back onto the left foot, releasing the toe of the front foot.

Continue into the Impetus or Open Impetus Turn.

The Impetus Turn

1

COUNT – SLOW

Man Walk forward onto the right foot starting to turn right and swing the left foot forward along the zig.

Woman Walk back onto the left foot, starting to turn right.

Man's Sway – straight-right-right, straight-left-straight
Woman's Sway – straight-left-left, straight-right-straight

Cornering

In your Short Programme, you should aim to dance into a corner using the Impetus Turn. As you exit the corner, the man will be on the zag of the new wall, backing the centre line. As you start your Short Programme again, the couple will need to make a quarter turn (90°) to the left over Steps 1-2 of the Feather Finish.

2

COUNT – QUICK

Man Transfer the body weight onto the toes of the left foot turning right to end backing along the room.

Woman Pull the right heel back in contact with the floor to close to the left foot. On the left heel and with the feet together, make a three-eighths turn (135°) to the right to end facing along the room and lift onto the toes of the right foot.

3

COUNT – QUICK

Man Walk back onto the right foot, lowering toe-heel.

Woman Walk forward onto the left foot, in-line with the man, lowering toe-heel.

4

COUNT – SLOW

Man Walk back onto the left foot, starting to turn right.

Woman Walk forward onto the right foot, starting to turn right and swing the left foot forward past the man.

zag of new wall or zig of same wall

WALL

FLOW

zig

Improving the Smoothness

Many dancers' desire to dance well is translated into physical effort. Try to keep the dance relaxed and avoid over-dancing. The length of the steps is important in maintaining smoothness. Generally, over three steps, the relative length of the steps will be short-long-short, corresponding to a step-swing-step-step action. On the first step, the slow count, the dancer takes a step and develops the swing by moving the other foot ready for the second step on the quick count. The swing is resolved and neutralized in Step 3 as it moves from acting on one side of the body to the other. In some moves, such as a heel turn (Steps 1-3 Impetus Turn as woman, or Steps 4-6 as man), the person dancing the heel turn cannot take a long second step, but the other person will.

5

COUNT – QUICK

Man Pull the right heel back in contact with the floor, to close to the left foot. On the left heel and with the feet together, make a three-eighths turn (135°) to the right to end on the zag facing the centre line of the room and lift onto the toes of the right foot.

Woman Still turning right, transfer the body weight sideways onto the toes of the left foot and bring the right back to touch or brush the side of the left foot completing a three-eighths turn (135°) to end on the zag, backing the centre line.

6

COUNT – QUICK

Man Continuing to turn on the right foot, step to the side and slightly back lowering the body weight, toe-heel, onto the left foot to end on the zig, backing the centre line.

Woman Still turning on the toes of the left foot, step diagonally forward onto the right foot, lowering toe-heel, to end on the zig, facing the centre line.

Continue with the Feather Finish.

This Short Programme, consisting of the Feather Finish – Three Step – Impetus Turn, can then be repeated and danced continuously. The angles of the zigs and zags can be adjusted to provide more or less progression around the floor and to gauge the approach to a corner.

Reverse Turn

In dancing, a "reverse" turn simply means a turn made to the left. We can introduce the Reverse Turn directly into your Short Programme. Start by dancing the Feather Finish just as before but turning it a quarter turn (90°) to the left, to end with the man on the zag facing the centre line. You are now ready to dance the Reverse Turn.

1

COUNT – SLOW

Man Walk forward onto the left foot in-line with the woman, starting to turn left and swing the right foot forward along the zag.

Woman Walk back onto the right foot, starting to turn left.

2

COUNT – QUICK

Man Transfer the body-weight forward onto the toes of the right foot, turning left to end backing along the room.

Woman Pull the left heel back in contact with the floor, to close to the right foot. On the right heel and with the feet together, turn to end facing along the room and lift onto the toes of the left foot.

3

COUNT – QUICK

Man Walk back onto the left foot, lowering toe-heel.

Woman Walk forward onto the right foot, in-line with the man, lowering toe-heel.

> *Man's Sway – straight-left-left, straight-right-right*
> *Woman's Sway – straight-right-right, straight-left-left*

4

COUNT – SLOW

Man Walk back onto the right foot, starting to turn left and swing the left foot back.

Woman Walk forward onto the left foot, starting to turn left and swing the right foot forward.

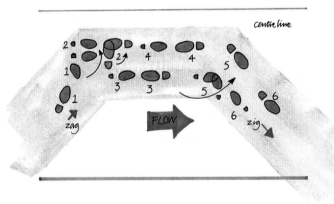

5

COUNT – QUICK

Man Transfer the body weight sideways onto the toes of the left foot onto the zig.

Woman Transfer the body weight sideways onto the right foot, toe-heel, still turning to the left.

6

COUNT – QUICK

Man Step forward with the right foot outside the woman's right side, lowering, toe-heel, on the zig.

Woman Walk back onto the left foot, a little under the body, moving back along the zig towards the wall.

> *You are now in the same position as you originally were at the end of the Feather Finish. Continue with the Three Step, the Reverse Wave or the Hover Telemark.*

Natural Weave

An excellent Slow Foxtrot figure which enables the dancers to change direction quickly and move along the floor out of traffic problems is the Natural Weave. It is danced after the Three Step. The man is standing on his left foot on the zig, ready to move towards the wall. The woman is standing on her right foot.

1

COUNT – SLOW

Man Walk forward onto the right foot, starting to turn right.

Woman Walk back onto the left foot, starting to turn right.

2

COUNT – QUICK

Man Move sideways onto the toes of the left foot, making nearly a quarter turn (90°) to the right onto the zag.

Woman Pull the right heel back in contact with the floor to close to the left foot. On the left heel and with the feet together, make a quarter turn (90°) to the right and lift onto the toes of the right foot.

> Man's Sway – straight-right-straight, left-straight-right-right
> Woman's Sway – straight-left-straight, right-straight-left-left

Combining the Figures for Different Dance Floors

By dancing the Short Programme, the Extended Programme which includes the Reverse Turn, and the Natural Weave, you will soon learn how far around the room each series of moves will take you. You can now build your experience by practising various combinations to suit the size of any dance floor. For example, on a medium-size rectangular floor, you might start at the beginning of a long side and dance the Extended Programme including the Reverse Turn, to arrive two-thirds of the way along the long side. The Short Programme would then complete the long side and another Short Programme would take you across the short side. Alternatively, the long side might consist of the Feather Finish – Reverse Turn – Three Step – Natural Weave – Three Step – Impetus Turn.

3

COUNT – QUICK

Man Move back onto the toes of the right foot along the zag, allowing the body to turn to face almost against the flow.

Woman Move forward onto the toes of the left foot along the zag, allowing the body to turn to face almost along the room.

4

COUNT – QUICK

Man Move back underneath the body onto the toes of the left foot.

Woman Move forward and a little across yourself onto the toes of the right foot, to step along the zag outside the man's right side.

5

COUNT – QUICK

Man Move back onto the toes of the right foot, starting to turn left.

Woman Move forward onto the toes of the left foot, starting to turn left.

6

COUNT – QUICK

Man Move sideways onto the toes of the left foot, turning onto the zig.

Woman Move sideways onto the right foot, still turning left, toe-heel.

7

COUNT – SLOW

Man Step forward onto the right foot outside the woman, lowering toe-heel.

Woman Move the left foot back slightly underneath the body along the zig.

Continue with the
Three Step, Reverse Wave or Hover Telemark.

The Curved Three Step

The Three Walks Curving to Left used in the Waltz can also be danced in the Slow Foxtrot instead of Steps 1-3 of the Reverse Turn. Use the standard Slow-Quick-Quick timing and continue with Steps 4-6 of the Reverse Turn. It is also a very good entry, if underturned, to the Reverse Wave, omitting Steps 1-3 of the Reverse Turn.

Reverse Wave

The Reverse Wave is one of the most elegant and versatile moves in the Slow Foxtrot. A nice combination is to dance the Curved Three Step, underturning it so that the man ends backing along a zig. The standard entry for the Reverse Wave, though, is to dance it immediately after the Reverse Turn. This superb combination uses some of the moves with which you are already familiar. Start by dancing the Reverse Turn. Then, dance Steps 1-3 of the Reverse Turn, again starting with the man facing the wall on the zig and over-turning the move to half a turn, to end with the man backing the wall on the zig. The extra amount of turn can make this move a little tricky. It is important for the woman to take a small step on Step 1 and for the man not to try to rush or force the turn.

1

COUNT – SLOW

Man Walk back onto the right foot, starting to curve to the left.

Woman Walk forward onto the left foot and swing the right foot forward, starting to curve to the left.

2

COUNT – QUICK

Man Walk back onto the toes of the left foot, continuing to curve to the left.

Woman Transfer the body-weight forward onto the right foot and lift from the heel onto the toes of the right foot, continuing a gradual curve to the left.

3

COUNT – QUICK

Man Walk back onto the right foot, completing the curve to the left to end backing along the room.

Woman Lower the body weight stepping forward, toe-heel, onto the left foot, completing the curve to the left to end facing along the room.

> *Man's Sway – straight-right-right*
> *Woman's Sway – straight-left-left*

> *Continue with Steps 4-6 of the Impetus Turn or the Open Impetus Turn. You can also dance the Natural Turn.*

The Feather Step

Many dancers often use the Feather Step to start the Slow Foxtrot and as an entry into the Reverse Turn. The man is standing on his left foot on a zag, facing the centre-line of the room. The woman is standing on her right foot on a zag, backing the centre line of the room.

1

COUNT – SLOW

Man Walk forward onto the right foot and swing the left foot forward along the zag.

Woman Walk back onto the left foot and start to move the right foot back, releasing the toe first.

2

COUNT – QUICK

Man Allow the swing to continue to bring the body-weight onto the toes of the left foot, and to turn the body a little to the right.

Woman Walk back onto the right foot and start to move the left foot back, releasing the toe first and allowing the body to turn slightly to right.

3

COUNT – QUICK

Man Step forward and slightly across onto the right foot outside the woman's right side, and lower toe-heel.

Woman Walk back and slightly underneath the body onto the left foot and start to move the right foot back, releasing the toe first.

> *Man's Sway – straight-right-right*
> *Woman's Sway – straight-left-left*

> *Continue into the Reverse Turn, Curved Three Step, the Open Telemark or the Quick Open Reverse Turn variations.*

The Natural Turn at a Corner

When the Feather Step is used to start the Slow Foxtrot, a move called the Natural Turn is often used at a corner as a way of getting into it. The Natural Turn can be used instead of the Impetus Turn. First, as you approach the corner, dance Steps 1-3 of the Impetus Turn. The man is now backing along the room and is back on his right foot. The woman is facing along the room and is forward on her left foot.

1
COUNT – SLOW

Man Walk back onto the left foot, starting to pull the right heel back in contact with the floor.

Woman Walk forward onto the right foot.

The couple should stay down over these three steps and should avoid rushing the three "slow" counts of the move.

2
COUNT – SLOW

Man Keeping the feet a little apart, pull the right foot to the side and, making one-eighth of a turn (45°) to the right, end standing on the right foot facing along the zag of the new wall, towards the centre line.

Woman Move sideways onto the left foot, turning a little to right, and drag the right foot to touch the left foot.

> *Man's Sway – straight-left-straight*
> *Woman's Sway – straight-right-straight*

3
COUNT – SLOW

Man Walk forward onto the left foot along the zag, towards the centre line.

Woman Walk back onto the right foot.

Combining the Natural Turn with Other Moves

You can now continue with a Feather Step at the beginning of the new side. It is also possible to miss out the last step of the Natural Turn and dance straight into the Reverse Turn or the Curved Three Step. A nice combination is to dance Steps 1-2 of the Natural Turn, to end at the beginning of the new side. Then dance Steps 1-3 of the Reverse Turn, making only a quarter of a turn (90°), to end with the man backing along the zig. Follow straight into the Reverse Wave.

The Natural Turn can also be danced along the side of the room using three-eighths of a turn (135°), to end with the man facing along the zag towards the centre line. You would then follow the move with any of the combinations recommended above.

The Open Telemark

The Open Telemark is a very elegant and satisfying way of moving into Promenade Position in the Slow Foxtrot. It is also a very useful way of changing direction towards the wall, but still moving along the room instead of dancing a Reverse Turn. Start with the man on the zag, facing the centre line of the room. The man is standing on the right foot and the woman her left foot.

1

COUNT – SLOW

Man Transfer the body-weight forward onto the toes of the right foot, turning left to end backing along the zag.

Woman Pull the left heel back in contact with the floor to close to the right foot. On the right heel and with the feet together, turn to end facing along the room, and lift onto the toes of the left foot. Start to move the head over to the right.

Man's Sway – straight-left-straight
Woman's Sway – straight-right-straight

2

COUNT – QUICK

Man Walk forward onto the left foot in-line with the woman, starting to turn left, and swing the right foot forward along the zag.

Woman Walk back onto the right foot, starting to turn left.

3

COUNT – QUICK

Man Point the left foot along the zig and lower onto it, toe-heel, in Promenade Position.

Woman Point the right foot along the zig and lower onto it, toe-heel, in Promenade Position with the head to the right.

Continue with either a Feather Ending from Promenade Position or a Passing Natural Turn. The Open Telemark can also be overturned to end along the room. Follow with the Wing and Syncopated Progressive Chassé to the right and the Weave Ending, ended facing along the zig towards the wall.

The Feather Ending from Promenade Position

This is a very practical exit from Promenade Position which should be in everyone's Slow Foxtrot repertoire. Start in Promenade Position, having danced, for example, an Open Telemark.

Man's Sway – straight-right-right
Woman's Sway – straight-left-left

1

COUNT – SLOW

Man Walk forward and across onto the right foot along the zig and in Promenade Position, starting to swing the left foot forward.

Woman Walk forward and across onto the left foot along the zig and in Promenade Position, starting to turn to the left.

2

COUNT – QUICK

Man Transfer the body weight forward onto the toes of the left foot, moving along the zig.

Woman Move sideways onto the right foot, continuing to turn towards the man.

3

COUNT – QUICK

Man Step forward and slightly across onto the right foot outside the woman's right side, and lower toe-heel.

Woman Move back onto the left foot, slightly underneath the body and completing the turn to face the man.

> *Continue with the Three Step or Reverse Wave, remembering to dance steps 1–3 of the Reverse Turn.*

The Passing Natural Turn

The Passing Natural Turn is the standard entry for the classy Outside Swivel and a range of other moves which your dance coach would be pleased to show you. First, dance the Open Telemark as described earlier then follow it with the Passing Natural Turn.

1

COUNT – SLOW

Man Walk forward and across onto the right foot in Promenade Position, along the zig, starting to turn to the right, to end facing along the zag towards the wall. Swing the left foot forward towards the zag.

Woman Walk forward and across onto the left foot along the zig and in Promenade Position.

> *It will feel a little as though the man is cutting across the woman but he should avoid impeding the woman's progress along the zig.*

> *Man and Woman – No Sway*

2

COUNT – QUICK

Man Move the body weight forward onto the toes of the left foot and continue turning, to back along the room.

Woman Move forward along the zig, between the man's feet, onto the toes of the right foot.

3

COUNT – QUICK

Man Move back, lowering toe-heel, onto the right foot along the zig towards the wall, bringing the right side of the body back with the right foot.

Woman Step forward, along the zig, lowering toe-heel onto the left foot, bringing the left side of the body forward with the left foot.

> *Continue into the Outside Swivel.*

The Outside Swivel

The stylish move continues from the Open Telemark and Passing Natural Turn combination. It is a standard and popular Slow Foxtrot figure which I am confident you will enjoy.

1

COUNT – SLOW

Man Move back along the zig, slightly underneath the body, onto the left foot with the toe turned inwards. Allow the right foot to cross loosely in front of the left foot, still in contact with the floor. On the left foot, swivel a quarter turn (90°) to the right to end on the zag towards the centre line. Lead the woman to turn right to end in Promenade Position.

Woman Walk forward and across onto the right foot along the zig and outside the man's right side. Bring the left foot to the right foot and, on the right foot, swivel to the right to end on the zag towards the centre line. Don't rush this step.

> *Man and Woman – No Sway*

> *Continue with the Feather Ending from Promenade Position moving along the zag towards the centre line, or with the Weave or the Wing.*

The Open Impetus Turn

You have already been enjoying the Impetus Turn as part of your basic Slow Foxtrot. Now we introduce some modifications to end the figure in Promenade position, and give an opportunity to develop extra style in the shape of the move. The Open Impetus Turn is danced along the side of the room. Start by dancing Steps 1-3 of the Impetus Turn.

4

COUNT – SLOW

Man Walk back onto the left foot, starting to turn right.

Woman Walk forward onto the right foot, starting to turn right and swing the left foot forward past the man.

5

COUNT – QUICK

Man Pull the right heel back in contact with the floor to close to the left foot. On the left heel and with the feet together, make a three-eighths turn (135°) to the right to end on the zag, facing the centre line of the room, and lift onto the toes of the right foot.

Woman Still turning right, transfer the body weight sideways onto the toes of the left foot and bring the right back to touch or brush the side of the left foot on the zag.

> *Man's Sway – straight-right-straight*
> *Woman's Sway – straight-left-straight*

6

COUNT – QUICK

Man Continuing to turn on the right foot to face along the room, take a small step along the zag towards the centre line, lowering the body-weight, toe-heel, onto the left foot in Promenade Position.

Woman Still turning on the toes of the left foot, take a small step onto the toes of the right foot along the zag towards the centre line, then lower, toe-heel, onto the right foot in Promenade Position.

Continue with the Feather Ending, the Weave or the Wing. If danced at a corner, it is possible to dance straight into a Passing Natural Turn and Outside Swivel at the beginning of the new side.

Using your Head

Normally, the man's head will remain to the left. However, to add extra style, the man may look to the right over the woman's left shoulder as he sways and turns to the right on Steps 4 and 5. As the couple lift onto the toes, the man and the woman will synchronize the movement of their heads into Promenade Position.

4a

COUNT – SLOW

5a

COUNT – QUICK

The Weave

The Weave has become one of the International Standard moves in the Slow Foxtrot and this version is designed to be danced after the Open Impetus Turn or the Outside Swivel. The couple are in Promenade Position ready to move along the zag towards the centre line. The man is standing on the left foot and the woman on the right foot.

1
COUNT – SLOW

Man Walk forward and across onto the right foot along the zag towards the centre line in Promenade Position.

Woman Walk forward and across onto the left foot along the zag, towards the centre line, in Promenade Position.

2
COUNT – QUICK

Man Take a small step forward onto the toes of the left foot along the zag between the woman's feet, starting to turn to the left.

Woman Turning to left across the man, move sideways onto the toes of the right foot, backing the centre line along the zag.

Man's Sway – straight-straight-left-left, straight-right-right
Woman's Sway – straight-straight-right-right, straight-left-left

3
COUNT – QUICK

Man Move sideways onto the toes of the right foot, turning left to end backing the zig towards the wall.

Woman Move sideways onto the the toes of the left foot, turning to the left to face down the room.

4
COUNT – QUICK

Man Move back onto the toes of the left foot slightly underneath the body, turning to back down the room.

Woman Step forward and across outside the man's right side, onto the toes of the right foot.

5
COUNT – QUICK

Man Move back onto the toes of the right foot, backing down the room, still turning to the left.

Woman Step forward onto the toes of the left foot in-line with the man, and continuing to turn to the left.

6

COUNT – QUICK

Man Still turning to the left, point the left foot along the zig and transfer the body weight onto the toes of the left foot.

Woman Move sideways onto the right foot, turning left to back the wall.

7

COUNT – QUICK

Man Step forward and across onto the toes of the right foot on the zig, outside the woman's right side, and lower toe-heel.

Woman Move back slightly underneath the body onto the left foot, along the zig towards the wall.

> *Continue with the Three Step, Steps 1–3 of the Reverse Turn & Reverse Wave or the Hover Telemark.*

The Wing and Syncopated Progressive Chassé to Right with a Weave Ending

The best dancers always have an alternative move ready to dance should the way ahead become blocked by other floor traffic. Imagine you have just danced an Open Impetus Turn or an Outside Swivel, and you are unable to move towards the centre line because of other floor traffic. Now is the time to dance the Wing in which the man halts the couple's progress to lead the woman to dance three walks around him, to finish on his left side – the opposite to normal – now that's Floorcraft with Flair!

The Wing

1

COUNT – SLOW

Man Walk forward and across onto the right foot in Promenade Position along the zag towards the centre-line, starting to turn to the left.

Woman Walk forward onto the left foot, starting to turn left around the man.

> *Man's Sway – straight-right-right*
> *Woman's Sway – straight-left-left*

Style Tip
As the woman walks around the man, it is important for her to keep her right side forward to maintain contact with the man. The woman gradually turns her head to the left over the move.

2

COUNT – QUICK

Man Standing on the right foot, swivel slowly to the left, drawing the left foot in contact with the floor towards the right foot but without putting any weight onto the left foot.

Woman Walk forward onto the toes of the right foot, continuing to move around the man.

3

COUNT – QUICK

Man Still on the right foot, continue to swivel to left to complete a quarter turn (90°) drawing the left foot to close to the right foot without weight. End standing on the right foot.

Woman Lowering toe-heel onto the left foot, walk forward between yourself and the man's left side.

Continue with the Syncopated Progressive Chassé to Right.

The Syncopated Progressive Chassé to Right

While a Chassé is a common figure in the Waltz and Quickstep, it is less common in the Slow Foxtrot. This gives the move a degree of surprise and adds a little unexpected highlight in the middle of the combination. The Chassé moves along the zag towards the centre-line of the room.

Man and Woman – No Sway

1

COUNT – SLOW

Man Walk forward onto the left foot outside the woman's left side, starting to turn to the left and swing the right foot along the zag.

Woman Move back onto the right foot, starting to turn left and swing the left foot back along the zag.

2

COUNT – QUICK

Man Move sideways onto the toes of the right foot along the zag, still turning to the left.

Woman Move sideways onto the toes of the left foot along the zag, still turning to the left.

3

COUNT – &

Man Close the toes of the left foot to the toes of the right foot still turning to the left.

Woman Close the toes of the right foot to the toes of the left foot still turning to the left.

4

COUNT – QUICK

Man Move sideways and slightly back onto the toes of the right foot along the zag, still turning to the left to back down the room.

Woman Move to the side and slightly forward onto the toes of the left foot along the zag, still turning left to face down the room.

Continue with Steps 4-7 of the Weave.

The Quick Open Reverse Turn with Turning Cross

The Quick Open Reverse Turn

The Quick Open Reverse Turn is a standard move in itself. To dance the basic Quick Open Reverse Turn, dance Steps 1-3 of the figure as described below, then Steps 5-7 of the Weave.

The Quick Open Reverse Turn with Turning Cross

We are now going to upgrade the Quick Open Reverse Turn to climax with a crossing action. I always associate this move with my one time coach, former World Ballroom Champion, Len Armstrong, whose powerful movement and control perfectly suited this figure. I hope it suits you too. Start as if ready to dance the standard Reverse Turn.

Man's Sway – straight-left-left, straight-right-right
Woman's Sway – straight-right-right, straight-left-left

1

COUNT – SLOW

Man Walk forward onto the left foot in-line with the woman and along the zag, towards the centre line, starting to turn left and swing the right foot forward along the zag.

Woman Walk back onto the right foot along the zag towards the centre line, starting to turn left, and swing the left foot back along the zag.

2

COUNT – QUICK

Man Transfer the body weight forward onto the toes of the right foot, turning left to end backing along the zig.

Woman Point the toes of the left foot along the room and transfer the body weight onto the toes of the left foot, turning to the left.

3

COUNT – &

Man Move back underneath the body onto the toes of the left foot, continuing to turn left to back down the room.

Woman Step forward and across onto the toes of the right foot, along the room and outside the man's right side.

4

COUNT – QUICK

Man Move back onto the right foot, turning to back along the zag towards the centre line, and lowering momentarily.

Woman Move forward onto the left foot in-line with the man, turning to the left on the zag towards the centre line and lowering momentarily.

5

COUNT – SLOW

Man Point the toes of the left foot along the room, and turning to face along the zig, transfer the body weight onto the toes of the left foot.

Woman Move sideways onto the toes of the right foot, still turning to the left to end backing the zig.

6

COUNT – &

Man Cross the right foot, lowering it behind the left foot and continue turning to end facing along the room.

Woman Cross the left foot, lowering it in front of the right foot and continue turning, to end backing down the room.

> *Continue with the Open Telemark, which you will need to turn a little more than normal, or underturn the Quick Open Reverse Turn with Turning Cross, to end facing along the zig towards the wall, and dance the Hover Telemark.*

The Hover Telemark

The Hover Telemark is a super move in both the Waltz and Slow Foxtrot. It is described in the Waltz section, but you can dance it in exactly the same way in the Slow Foxtrot, using the standard Slow Foxtrot timing of Slow-Quick-Quick.

> *Continue with the Passing Natural & Outside Swivel or Feather Ending in Promenade Position.*

Viennese Waltz

The elegance and charm of the Viennese Waltz conjures up spectacular images of gracious balls in the great houses and palaces of the European nobility, yet the Waltz started life as the "Ländler", an Austrian folkdance. The Viennese Waltz continues as a specified dance in Championship competitions, where the competitors exhibit their graceful fluency, stamina and control at speed, as they rotate around the floor to a quick tempo of 60 bars per minute.

Despite this image of a fast, dizzy and demanding dance, the Waltz never lost its common appeal and versions of it remain among the most popular of social dances, particularly in Europe.

Here, we explore the simplified social version, which is neither strenuous nor vertigo-inducing. For social dancers, the Waltz is transformed into a beautiful, lilting version which everyone can enjoy, whatever their level of ability.

In the Championship version of the Viennese Waltz, the competitors dance one step to each beat of music. In this popular social version, the simple moves comprise one gentle swing action to each bar of music, giving the dance the delightful lilting feel but without the speed of its competition counterpart. The dance should still progress around the room, albeit at a gentler pace.

Basic Natural Lilt Step

Start on a zig. The man is standing on his left foot, feet together, while the woman is standing on her right foot, feet together. Each step starts on the first beat of each new bar of music and the move is taken over the whole bar. The next step is therefore taken on the first beat of the following bar of music.

1

Man Walk forward with the right foot, starting to turn to the right. Allow the left foot to swing forward towards the right foot.

Woman Walk back with the left foot, starting to turn right. Allow the right foot to swing back towards the left foot.

2

Man Walk back with the left foot, continuing to turn right. Allow the right foot to swing back towards the left foot.

Woman Walk forward with the right foot, continuing to turn to the right. Allow the left foot to swing forward towards the right foot.

The Basic Natural Lilt Step can be repeated several times so that a gradual turn to the right is made.

Basic Reverse Lilt Step

This move gradually turns the dancers to the left. It is conventionally started when the man is on a zag, ready to move forward towards the centre line of the room. The man is standing on his right foot, having completed a Basic Natural Lilt Step, and the woman is standing on her left foot.

1

Man Walk forward with the left foot, starting to turn to the left. Allow the right foot to swing forward towards the left foot.

Woman Walk back with the right foot, starting to turn left. Allow the left foot to swing back towards the right foot.

2

Man Walk back with the right foot, continuing to turn left. Allow the left foot to swing back towards the right foot.

Woman Walk forward with the left foot, continuing to turn left. Allow the right foot to swing forward towards the left foot.

The Basic Reverse Lilt Step can be repeated several times so that a gradual turn to the left is made. It is conventional to complete the series of Basic Reverse Lilt Steps on a zig so that the Basic Natural Lilt Step may follow.

Stationary Lilt Step

It is always important to be courteous to other dancers on the floor and good dancers will always give way to less experienced ones. It may therefore be good practice temporarily to interrupt your progress in deference to other floor traffic. This is simple with the Stationary Lilt Step, which is danced on the spot with a sideways lilting action. It may be danced as often as is necessary, and in any position, before continuing with the original desired move. The move can start with either foot, but here we shall try it starting with the man's right foot. Start therefore as for the Basic Natural Lilt Step.

1

Man Move sideways on to the right foot, allowing the left foot to swing towards the right foot.

Woman Move sideways on to the left foot, allowing the right foot to swing towards the left foot.

2

Man Move sideways on to the left foot, allowing the right foot to swing towards the left foot.

Woman Move sideways on to the right foot, allowing the left foot to swing towards the right foot.

Sequence Dancing

Sequence Dancing is very popular in the UK, and in Australia, where it is called New Vogue dancing. Old Time Sequence dances employ the old ballet feet positions. Modern Sequence dances are based on Modern or Standard Ballroom dances, and Latin-American Sequence dances are based on the Latin-American dances. Each dance is generally choreographed into a standard 16-bar routine. Each routine or sequence is given a name; this becomes the dance, which may be repeated several times during the piece of music. The dancers all start at the same time and dance the same sequence of moves until the music ends. Sequence Dancing tends to reduce the need for technique and leading and is particularly popular with older social dancers, who enjoy the music and social atmosphere without the need to work at producing a high level of dancing. There is a constant supply of new dances, so when the dancers become bored with one they simply move on to another.

One of the drawbacks, though, is that there are now tens of thousands of Sequence dances listed, and different Sequence Dance clubs may share only a few dances in their common repertoire. If you plan to go to a Sequence Dance club or to go on a Sequence Dance holiday, check first which dances will be played. It is not acceptable to dance any dance other than the one that has been announced. As a reminder, most Sequence Dance "leaders" will first dance the sequence through before the dancers themselves take to the floor. Sequence dances that have become classics include the "Mayfair Quickstep", the "Saunter Together", the "Tango Serida", the "Melody Foxtrot" and the "Square Tango".

To exit, there are four options:

1 When the man is standing on his left foot, exit forwards with the Basic Natural Lilt Step.

2 When the man is standing on his left foot, exit backwards with Step 2 of the Basic Reverse Lilt Step.

3 When the man is standing on his right foot, exit forwards with Basic Reverse Lilt Step.

4 When the man is standing on his right foot, exit backwards with Step 2 of the Basic Natural Lilt Step.

Jive from Lindy Hop to Rock 'n' Roll

Dance styles have always followed musical trends and none more so than the dance which was to become Rock 'n' Roll. While we tend to think of the Rock 'n' Roll phenomenon as beginning in the 1950s, the dance actually started emerging more than two decades earlier in the USA. During the early 1920s, there had been a veritable zoo of animal dances, the best known of which was probably the Turkey Trot. These were in addition to other dance crazes, such as the Charleston and Black Bottom, whose wild moves got wilder as the music got faster. Other dances and styles developed from these and the Texas Tommy or Breakaway, in which the couple moved apart and came back together, emerged during the 1920s.

The Lindy Hop and Jitterbug

By the end of the decade, this style was extremely popular. In 1927, when Charles Lindbergh piloted the Spirit of St Louis solo across the Atlantic, the newspaper headlines declaring this event were adopted as the new name for the dance, the Lindy Hop. As the dance continued to develop into the 1930s, it found a home in the Harlem Savoy Ballroom, where it grew up with the great Swing bands of the era. The line-up of orchestras who played at the Harlem Savoy sounds like a Who's Who of Swing. Benny Goodman, Cab Calloway, Tommy Dorsey, Louis Armstrong, Count Basie and Duke Ellington all performed at the Savoy. The bands inspired the dancers and the dancers inspired the bands in an upward-reaching spiral towards new heights of dance and musical expression.

When Benny Goodman gave a concert at the Paramount Theatre, New York, in 1937, teenagers went wild and poured into the aisles to "Jitterbug", as the newspapers called the dance. The craze swept

Above: The Lindy Hop originated in the late 1920s after Charles Lindburgh's transatlantic flight. It developed and gained in popularity throughout the 1930s and 1940s.

Right: The spirit of fifties Rock 'n' Roll is as popular as ever in specialist clubs and classes.

across America. Variations in technique led to styles such as Boogie-woogie and Swing Boogie, with "Jive" gradually emerging as the generic term that covered Lindy Hop, Jitterbug and Boogie-woogie dances. Whichever term was used in the 1940s, the music was Swing.

Dance Styles – Lindy Hop to Rock 'n' Roll

After the Second World War, bands got smaller and the music changed. By the 1950s, the music was no longer as smooth and polished as Swing but it had huge popular appeal; this music was Rock 'n' Roll. With the change in music came a change in the dancers' interpretation of the music. The heavier beat engendered a more two-dimensional jive with a "choppier" feel. By the end of the 1950s, jive had already reached the ballrooms and dance schools but in a different style.

The basis of all the dances from the Lindy Hop, through Boogie-woogie to Rock 'n' Roll is virtually the same: a six-beat musical rhythm (though the Lindy Hop also used an eight-beat rhythm). In the basic dance, the dancers take two steps which rock or swing sideways, then a step backwards and a replace step. The step backwards and replace movement remained fairly standard, as it gave the dances their rhythmic point of reference. However, the sideways rock or swing steps underwent many changes of style.

In Boogie-woogie, a tap is often added to make the sequence: tap, step, tap, step, step back, replace. The steps are danced well down into the knees.

In Rock 'n' Roll competitions, the Boogie taps became flicks in the sequence: flick, step, flick, step, step back, replace. This style has become quite extreme in dance competitions, with routines of dazzling acrobatic moves interspersed with the more basic dance moves. While it is very impressive, this performance style owes more to acrobatic prowess than to the notion of a man and woman coming together to dance. Most dancers prefer to dance to good music for their own enjoyment, which is the focus of this section, leaving the performance hybrid of Rock 'n' Roll to others.

The figures or moves introduced in this book are described without flicks or taps, with a basic style reminiscent of Lindy Hop. When you have practised and are confident with the basic steps, you can add the Rock 'n' Roll flicks or the Boogie taps if you prefer. Rock 'n' Roll is danced more upright because of the flicking action, while the Boogie style calls for very flexed knees.

Music Suggestions

As you learn the basic moves and begin to concentrate on perfecting your style, you will want to dance to the appropriate music. For Boogie-woogie fans, it would be hard to find better than "The Calloway Boogie" recorded in New York in 1940 by Cab Calloway and still available on the Giants of Jazz label or "Hamp's Boogie-Woogie" by Lionel Hampton & His Septet" available on the Living Traditions label. Louis Jordan's classic "Choo Choo Ch'Boogie" is on the Giants of Jazz label. Other artists to look out for are Count Basie, Memphis Slim, Joe Turner, Pete Johnson, Albert Ammons, Milt Buckner, Jay McShann and Sammy Price.

For Lindy Hoppers, swing is the thing and among many greats are "Posin'" by Jimmie Lunceford and Duke Ellington's "Let's Get Together". Glenn Miller's fabulous "In the Mood' and 'Tippin' In" by Erskine Hawkins are steady ones especially good for practice. These are all available on the Living Traditions label. Look for music by these artists plus Cab Calloway, Benny Goodman, Lionel Hampton, Count Basie and Artie Shaw on the Living Traditions and Giants of Jazz labels.

Rock 'n' Rollers will get moving to music of the 1950s. "Cincinatti Fireball" by Johnny Burnette (Liberty Records), is a steady number and a good one to start with. "See You Later Alligator" and "Shake, Rattle and Roll" by Bill Haley and His Comets (MCA) are two Rock 'n' Roll classics with steady tempos that are good for practice. When you have a little more confidence, "Tutti Frutti" by Little Richard (Specialty Records) starts with a medium tempo but picks up the pace. Most music of the 1950s with a steady 4/4 beat and a tempo ranging from 36-48 bars per minute will be suitable.

Getting Started

Initially, the most important thing is to get to grips with the rhythm. This is vital because, even when you and your partner know the moves, you will have to synchronize with each other to make the steps work and your cue is the rhythm. First, listen to some music, whether swing or Rock 'n' Roll is your preference. Swing and Rock 'n' Roll music has four beats to each bar of music. To start with, listen to the drum or rhythm line rather than to the melody. The drum provides the beat and you will notice that the drummer emphasizes beats 1 and 3 in each bar. You do not need to understand musical bars, just to be able to hear the all-important beat. A "quick" count equals one beat of music, while a "slow" count equals two beats. In a few figures, such as the Arm Breaker, two steps are danced to one beat of music. These are indicated by an "&" count, and are danced "quick, and" in the space of one beat.

The man and woman's roles are quite clearly defined. The man's job is generally to stay put, while the woman moves more around the floor. The roles of each can be summed up as follows:

The Man's Role:

• To keep the couple synchronized with the music and with each other. The woman must synchronize with the man, even if he is off-time with the music. This role is particularly important as an aid to the woman when she has completed a spin or turn and needs a point of reference to continue the dance in time with the music.

• To decide which figures to dance and in which order, leading the woman to dance them. Your main responsibility is to make your own moves clear and decisive to avoid confusing your partner. The lead should be clear and firm rather than strong and aggressive. The idea is to communicate the move to the woman rather than force her to dance it.

• To provide a point of orientation for the woman. While you stay mainly in place and the woman dances towards, around and away from you, it is easy for her to become disorientated. On completion of each move, she will be looking to orientate herself on your position before starting the next move. The man's steps are generally less difficult than the woman's, allowing you to "manage" the dance.

The Woman's Role:

• To be aware of the man's intentions as communicated by his lead and not to anticipate or guess moves. If you anticipate a move by committing your body weight in a certain direction too early, the man will have to revise his intentions, although he is in the worst position to do so. The resulting moves can be very awkward and clumsy.

• To check constantly that your rhythm is synchronized with that of the man and that you are orientating yourself in relation to him, particularly as a move ends. Check your rhythm on each "back, replace" step. If you are not synchronized with the man, don't try to slow down or speed up your next move to compensate. Just stop briefly and start again.

Couples should keep themselves from getting carried away by the music at the cost of getting the steps and rhythm wrong. More concentration is required in the learning stage but it will be amply rewarded when swinging from one figure to another becomes second nature to you. On the "back, replace" step, you should mostly be opposite your partner or sometimes side by side. Whichever it is, make sure that you are clearly in this position. If you are not and your partner decides to continue with a move requiring a strong lead, you may find your own body weight and impetus working against you, which can sometimes result in injuries such as a sprained wrist or jarred shoulder. Rock 'n' Roll and Jive are not in themselves dangerous dances but common sense should prevail.

The Basic Hold

There are a number of holds in Rock 'n' Roll dancing. The hold will depend on the preceding move, the current move and the following move. The transition from one type of hold to another should be quite natural. Tips on how to achieve this are given in the text as each change of hold is required.

To start the dance, face your partner with your feet slightly apart. The man stands with his weight on the right foot and the woman with her weight on the left foot. The man slips his right hand around the woman's waist, without drawing her too close to him. The woman rests her left hand comfortably on the man's upper right arm. Her right hand is held in the man's left hand, palm to palm and with her fingers between his fingers and thumb, her thumb curled around his thumb.

Use the basic hold to start off the dance, although you may use other holds as the dance progresses.

Basic Jive

In this introduction to Jive, the descriptions of the figures or moves will use the basic steps without flicks or taps. Later, when you have practised, you can add the Rock 'n' Roll flicks or the Boogie taps as preferred. In this basic move, it is essential that the knees remain quite flexed. Steps 3 and 4 are known as the "back, replace" steps and will be referred to often.

1

COUNT – SLOW

Man Rock to the side onto the left foot, taking a small step and leaving the right foot in place.

Woman Rock to the side onto the right foot, taking a small step and leaving the left foot in place.

2

COUNT – SLOW

Man Rock to the side onto the right foot, taking a small step and leaving the left foot in place.

Woman Rock to the side onto the left foot, taking a small step and leaving the right foot in place.

Style Tips

On Steps 1 and 2, you might like to sway a little in the direction of the step to improve the feeling. (For the man, this will also give a nice indication to the woman to move.) Do not use heels on any steps.

Try to keep the feet under the body during the moves to avoid creating excessive movement and making the dance difficult. Small steps are far more controlled than large ones.

Styling your Jive

The basic rock-rock-step-replace action of the Jive can be modified to suit your preferred style of Jive.

For the Lindy Hop and Jitterbug, incline the upper body slightly forward, moving the centre of the body weight further back in the seat. Dance the step, replace, by sliding the feet more in contact with the floor. Dance the rock, rock, steps as described.

For Boogie-woogie, assume the same posture as for Lindy Hop but with more flexing of the knees. On the rock to the left, the right toe will tap towards the left foot and, on the rock to the right, the left toe will tap towards the right foot.

For competition Rock 'n' Roll, assume an upright stance. On the rock to the left, the right foot will be flicked forward with a loose ankle and, on the rock to the right, the left foot will be flicked forward with a loose ankle. For informal social dancing, the flick is optional.

3

COUNT – QUICK

Man Rock onto the left foot, moving it under the body and placing the left toe behind the right heel. Lift the right foot just off the floor.

Woman Rock onto the right foot, moving it under the body and placing the right toe behind the left heel. Lift the left foot just off the floor.

4

COUNT – QUICK

Man Transfer your body weight forward onto the right foot.

Woman Transfer your body weight forward onto the left foot.

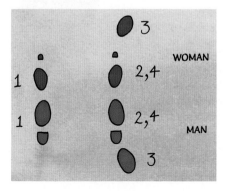

Repeat the Basic Jive as many times as you want as a useful way of practising dancing to the rhythm. The Basic Jive can also be turned gently in an anti-clockwise (counterclockwise) direction during Steps 1 and 2. At least four Basic Jives should be used to turn a full circle.

Throwaway

Experienced dancers will not use a set programme or routine, but before you get to that stage, it is useful to put together a practice programme. The Throwaway can be introduced immediately after the Basic Jive. The man dances the Basic Jive, turning on Steps 1 and 2 and leading the woman into an open position. Steps 3 and 4 remain the same.

1

COUNT – SLOW

Man Rock to the side onto the left foot, taking a small step and starting to turn to the left. Lead the woman to start to turn by bringing your left hand down to the left hip.

Woman Rock forward onto the right foot, towards the man's left side.

2

COUNT – SLOW

Man Rock to the side onto the right foot, taking a small step and completing a quarter turn (90°) to the left. Lead the woman into an open position by moving your left hand forward at waist height.

Woman Turn on the right foot to face the man and rock backwards onto the left foot away from the man into an open position.

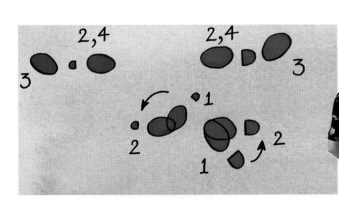

The Link
*From this position, dance the Basic Jive by moving towards your partner on the rock steps and resuming hold – this is called The Link.
Alternatively, try the Underarm Turn to the Right.*

3–4

COUNT – QUICK, QUICK

Man Dance Steps 3 and 4 of the Basic Jive (the back, replace steps).

Woman Dance Steps 3 and 4 of the Basic Jive.

Underarm Turn to the Right

This very popular figure features a turn to the right. The couple have danced the by now familiar rhythm of the Basic Jive and have just finished the back, replace steps. They are standing in an open position with a left hand to right hand hold. The man is standing on the right foot and the woman on the left foot.

1

COUNT – SLOW

Man Rock to the side onto the left foot, lifting the left arm to lead the woman to turn underneath.

Woman Turn underneath the man's left arm. Rock forward onto the right foot, starting to turn to the right.

2

COUNT – SLOW

Man Rock to the side onto the right foot, making a quarter turn (90°) to the left and returning the left hand to waist height.

Woman Rock to the side and back onto the left foot, continuing to turn to the right underneath the man's arm.

3–4

COUNT – QUICK, QUICK

Man Dance Steps 3 and 4 of the Basic Jive.

Woman Dance Steps 3 and 4 of the Basic Jive continuing the turn to end facing the man.

Practice Programme

You can now continue with a Link and the Basic Jive. The programme can be danced in the sequence: Rock Basic (dance several times, including a rotation to the left, if desired), Throwaway, Underarm Turn to the Right, Link, Basic Jive.

Comb

This figure has come to typify the Rock 'n' Roll style, despite the fact that it was already used 20 years before the Rock 'n' Roll era in the Lindy Hop. Teddy Boys were renowned for the care they took over their hair which involved frequent combing, hence the name of this classic figure. As usual, the couple have danced the back, replace steps. The man is now standing on the right foot and the woman on the left foot. The couple are in a right hand to right hand hold ready to dance the Comb.

1

COUNT – SLOW

Man Rock to the side onto the left foot towards the woman, lifting the right hands over your head as if combing your hair…

Woman Rock forward onto the right foot towards the man, allowing him to raise your right hand over his head…

Man …End with the right hand at your right shoulder.

Woman …It is comfortable to turn slightly to the left to a side-by-side position.

2

COUNT – SLOW

Man
Rock to the side onto the right foot away from the woman, releasing the right hand and allowing the woman's right hand to slip down your arm to your left hand, where you resume hold.

Woman Rock backwards onto the left foot, sliding the right hand down the man's left arm to resume hand hold.

Style Tip
While it is typical of 1950s-style Rock 'n' Roll for the man to lean back a little on Steps 1 and 2 of this move, the freer and more expressive style of Lindy Hop promoted much more personal interpretation, even allowing the man's upper body to incline much more forward during this move.

3–4

COUNTS – QUICK, QUICK

Man Dance the usual back, replace steps, resuming an open facing position.

Woman Dance the usual back, replace steps, resuming an open facing position. End standing on the left foot.

When practising, follow the Comb with a Link and resume your practice programme. If you want to start exploring other options, try following the Comb with the Underarm Turn to the Right.

Basic Turns

It is practical to intersperse basic turns between figures. There are a variety of turns which can be danced from either the basic hold or the open position.

Change of Place Right to Left
To dance the Change of Place Right to Left, start in the basic hold. Dance a Rock Basic and finish with the man on the right foot and the woman on the left foot, ready to go into this turn.

1

COUNT – SLOW

Man Rock to the side onto the left foot, raising the left arm to lead the woman to dance under your arm to the right. It is sometimes helpful to use the right hand to confirm to the woman that she is about to dance under your arm.

Woman Rock forward onto the right foot, starting to turn to the right.

2

COUNT – SLOW

Man Rock to the side onto the right foot, making a quarter turn (90°) to the left. End by lowering the left arm to waist height.

Woman Turning to the right under the man's arm, rock backwards onto the left foot to face the man.

Dance the back, replace steps, then continue with the Underarm Turn to the Right or dance the next figure.

Change of Place Left to Right

This figure retraces the path of the Change of Place Right to Left.

1
COUNT – SLOW

Man Rock to the side onto the left foot, raising the left arm to lead the woman across to your right.

Woman Rock forward onto the right foot, moving towards your left of the man.

2
COUNT – SLOW

Man Rock to the side onto the right foot, making a quarter turn to the right. End by lowering the left arm to a basic hold.

Woman Standing on the right foot, turn left under the man's arm to face him and rock to the side onto the left foot.

3–4
COUNT – QUICK, QUICK

Man Dance the back, replace steps, facing the woman in a basic hold.

Woman Dance the back, replace steps, facing the man in a basic hold.

Continue with a Link.

Change of Hands behind the Back

This stylish figure is not at all difficult if the guidelines are followed. Start as usual when you have just danced the standard back, replace steps and are in an open position.

1
COUNT – SLOW

Man Rock forward onto the left foot and place the woman's right hand into your right hand.

Woman Rock forward onto the right foot, aiming slightly towards the left of the man.

Changing Hands

It is the man's job to change hands when required by the next figure. The Change of Place Right to Left and Left to Right can both be concluded with either of the man's hands. If a turn under the arm has taken place, you should complete the change of hands at the end of the downward arm movement. Never let go of the woman's hand until you have placed it into your other hand.

2
COUNT – SLOW

Man Rock to the side onto the right foot, making a quarter turn to the left. Placing both hands behind your back, transfer the woman's right hand into your left hand. End with your back to the woman.

Woman Rock to the side onto the left foot, making a quarter turn to the right. End facing the man's back.

3–4
COUNT – QUICK, QUICK

Man Dance the back, replace steps, making a quarter turn to the left to end facing the woman in an open position.

Woman Dance the back, replace steps, making a quarter turn to the right to end facing the man in an open position.

Bringing Your Jive Alive

Now that you are familiar with some of the classic Jive and Rock 'n' Roll figures, you can concentrate on perfecting that style.

Suggested Programme
1 Basic Jive
2 Throwaway
3 Underarm Turn to the Right, ending in a right hand to right hand hold
4 Comb
5 Change of Hands behind the Back
6 Change of Place Left to Right
7 Link

• Generally keep the steps small. Remember that the objective is not to move around the floor.

• The man should try to avoid concentrating on what his partner is doing and should never follow her. Don't look at each other's feet. In many dances, when the woman steps backwards, the man steps forward. This is not the case in Jive, so it is far better to concentrate on your own steps and moves.

• Don't under any circumstances fudge the moves. Be accurate and clear.

• Maintain a steady rhythm and stick to it. The man should not, for example, hesitate to allow extra time for the woman to complete a turn.

• Don't be tempted to take short cuts. Women in particular must avoid turning too early. Learn the moves properly and you will quickly get them working for you instead of you working at them.

• Keep the movements compact. Avoid getting too far away from your partner, as this will make the dance uncomfortable and you may lose contact with each other.

Leading

You will already have picked up many useful and practical tips on leading through dancing the figures you have learned so far. Here are some further points to help you.

• In the open position, the man's hand should be palm uppermost with the woman's fingers held lightly between the man's palm and thumb.

• The man should always raise his arm high enough for the woman to turn beneath it comfortably, without having to duck.

• If the woman is turning in front of the man, both the man's and the woman's arm must be toned. The man leads the woman only by arm movements which are forward or backward in relation to his own hips, or by raising the arm. This causes the woman to pivot on her own foot and make the turn. The man's arm should never be extended with a view to pulling or pushing the woman.

• When the man leads the woman to turn or spin under his arm to the right using his right hand, the palm of the hand should first be rolled through 270° in the woman's hand until the two hands are again palm to palm. The back of the man's right hand will now be facing his body. If the right arm is now extended to a point above the woman's head and then lowered behind her head, she will automatically be led to turn. The man should decide how quickly to lower his arm in order to be in time with the rhythm of the music. The speed of lowering the arm has a direct effect on the speed of the woman's turn or spin.

Index